MAHAYANA BUDDHISM

BEATRICE LANE SUZUKI M.A.

With an Introduction by
Doctor D. T. Suzuki LITT.D.

and a Foreword by Christmas Humphreys

MANDALA
UNWIN PAPERBACKS
London   Boston   Sydney   Wellington

First published in 1938 by the Buddhist Lodge, London
Second edition in 1948 by David Matlowe Ltd
Third edition by George Allen & Unwin Ltd, in 1959
Fourth edition in 1981

First published in paperback by Unwin® Paperbacks, an imprint of
Unwin Hyman Limited in 1990.

© George Allen & Unwin Ltd, in 1981

The right of Beatrice Lane Suzuki to be identified as author of this work has
been asserted by her in accordance with the Copyrights, Designs and Patents
Act, 1988.

Unwin Hyman Limited
15–17 Broadwick Street, London W1V 1FP

Unwin Hyman, Inc.
8 Winchester Place, Winchester, MA 01890, USA

Allen & Unwin Australia Pty Ltd
8 Napier Street, North Sydney, NSW 2060, Australia

Allen & Unwin New Zealand Pty Ltd with the Port Nicholson Press
Compusales Building, 75 Ghuznee Street, Wellington, New Zealand

---

British Library Cataloguing in Publication Data

Suzuki, Beatrice Lane
Mahayana Buddhism. – 4th edition.
1. Mahayana Buddhism
I. Title
294.3′.92
ISBN 0-04-440594-4

Printed in Great Britain by Cox & Wyman Ltd, Reading

PRE

Foreword to Fourth Edition

The Buddhist Society was founded in London in 1924. At first the only Buddhism available was that of the Theravada, from Ceylon and Burma. Then came a series of works by Dr D. T. Suzuki on Zen Buddhism, beginning in 1927, and by the middle thirties a substantial number of works had appeared on the general field of Buddhism and, for the first time, Buddhist meditation. There was, however, nothing in the wide field of Mahayana Buddhism as such, save two large works by Dr D. T. Suzuki and Dr McGovern, which were both by then out of print. The Buddhist Society therefore sought to fill the gap, and as I had met Dr Suzuki in person in London in 1936 I wrote and asked for his help. He suggested that his wife, an American scholar who was particularly interested in the Shingon School but cognisant of the whole field of Japanese Buddhism, might write what was needed, and she at once agreed. In 1938 the Buddhist Society published in London the first edition of her work, *Mahayana Buddhism, A Brief Outline*, with a valuable Introduction by Dr Suzuki himself. Mrs Suzuki died in July 1939, and then came the war. The whole remaining stock of the first edition was destroyed in London in 1940, and all communication with Japan was cut in 1941.

In preparing the original work for a new edition I have re-read it in the light of my own later experience. In 1938 I received the manuscript from Mrs Suzuki as a description of the subject which I could not criticise, but in 1946 I spent six months in Japan, seeing a good deal of Dr Suzuki, and can therefore add a few words to Mrs Suzuki's account of Japanese Mahayana Buddhism.

While in Japan I got Dr Suzuki's help with a second edition of his late wife's work, which was published in London by David Marlowe Ltd. This edition was soon exhausted but, as there was still no brief work comparable with *Mahayana Buddhism*, the Society once more put this volume back in print, this time through George Allen & Unwin Ltd. This third edition now being exhausted, I have been asked to write a brief Introduction to the present fourth edition.

Being, as I found, widely known in Japan through the Buddhist Society's organ *The Middle Way*, I was welcomed at all levels of society, by professors and abbots, by village schoolmasters and artists, as well as by the aristocracy. I knew already of a dozen Buddhist schools of thought in Japan, but I was told to my surprise of many more. The differences between most of them could be easily digested, but those between the two main schools of *tariki*, 'salvation by another', and *jiriki*, 'self-salvation', were not to be ignored. I therefore sought for a common ground between them, and having with me a copy of 'Twelve Principles of Buddhism', drafted by the Buddhist Society in 1945 for the use of Western inquirers, I used them as an excuse to convene on a common platform representatives of the various sects. Committees were formed in Tokyo and Kyoto, and a Japanese translation agreed. Unimportant differences, largely of ritual or emphasis, were soon discarded, and after a while the formidable barrier of *tariki v. jiriki* alone prevented a complete acceptance of these Principles as the common denominator of Japanese Mahayana Buddhism. The Buddhism of the Southern School or *Theravada* is strongly *jiriki*. 'Work out your own salvation', said the Blessed One, according to the Pali Canon, 'and with diligence'. From this point of view the doctrine of *tariki*, salvation by some outside Power, is anathema. Where was the bridge on which these two might meet in concord?

The issue reached a critical stage at a meeting in the stronghold of the 'Pure Land' Sect, the Nishi Hongwanji Temple in Kyoto. The *tariki* pandits, in the presence of the hereditary Lord Abbot himself, disapproved of the phrase in our Principles which stressed 'self-salvation' as basic to the Buddhist way of life. I argued that 'the ways to the Goal are as many as the lives of men', and that both *tariki* and *jiriki* are in the long run means to an end, ways of 'working out one's own salvation'. In the end it was the Lord Abbot himself, a brilliant young man with a university degree, who suddenly announced: 'I agree with Mr Humphreys. *Tariki* and *jiriki* are both means to self-enlightenment.' And that was that. At a later meeting the seventeen major schools of Japanese Buddhism approved of the Principles, which therefore form today, at least in theory, the common basis of Japanese Mahayana Buddhism.

In Mrs Suzuki's text I have left the word Hinayana as a name for the oldest of the Buddhist Schools, although this pejorative epithet – meaning 'small vehicle' (of salvation) as distinct from the Mahayana, 'large vehicle' – has now been dropped in favour of the Theravada, meaning 'teaching of the Elders'. I have taken the responsibility of omitting parts of Chapter Four, on 'Mahayana in Practice'. After forty years much of the detail in it no longer applies, and in any case is only on the fringe of the wide field of Mahayana Buddhism. At the end of the book I have shortened Mrs Suzuki's own bibliography, and added a selection of more recent works which show the place of the Mahayana in the whole field of Buddhism.

As already stated, Mrs Suzuki died soon after completing this work, and Dr Suzuki himself died in 1966 at the age of ninety-five. All who study the vast field of Buddhism will remember them with gratitude for this brief but deeply helpful contribution to our Western knowledge of the Mahayana.

London, November 1980   CHRISTMAS HUMPHREYS

To all bodhisattvas in the world of
Samsara today
who are practising compassion
by working for human and animal
welfare

Contents

Foreword to Fourth Edition   page v

Preface   xi

Introduction by Doctor D. T. Suzuki   1

PART ONE

Chapter 1 Hinayana and Mahayana   21
Claim of Mahayana; Early History; Development of Mahayana;
Further Considerations of Hinayana and Mahayana

Chapter 2 1. Causation, Karma and Non-Ego   36
             2. The Buddhist Doctrine of Knowledge   37
             3. Tathata, Nirvana   39
The Mahayana doctrine of Tathata (Suchness); Sunyata and
Prajna; Nirvana

             4. Trikaya; The Three Bodies of The Buddha   48
Nirmanakaya; Sambhogakaya; Dharmakaya

             5. Amida   58
             6. Bodhisattva   61
             7. Enlightenment and Salvation   69

Chapter 3 Further Development of Mahayana   74

Chapter 4 Mahayana in Practice   77
Priests, monks and nuns; laymen; meditation

Chapter 5 Outline of Some Important Mahayana Sutras   83
Prajna Paramita; Avatamsaka; The Gandavyuha; Dasabhumika;
Vimalakirti Nirdesa; Surangama Samadhi; Saddharma Pundarika;
Srimaladevi; Brahmajala Sutra; Sukhavati Vyuha; Mahaparinir-
vana Sutra; The Lankavatara Sutra; Vajrasekhara Sutra; Kishin-
ron

PART TWO

Chapter 6 Extracts from Mahayana Sutras 103
General teaching of the Buddhas; True Nature of All Things;
The Mind; Transiency; Buddha-Nature; Mind Is the Origin of
Sin; Karma; Transmigration; The Origin of Ignorance; The Way
of Emancipation; Meditation; Modes of Wisdom; Buddha and
Compassion; The Buddha-Body; The Buddha-Field; Transmigra-
tin Is Nirvana; A Precept; Faith; Enlightenment; Repentance;
A Daily Precept; Root of Desire; Patience; Diligence; Chastity;
Gratitude; Master and Friend; Spirit of Charity; How to Behave
in this Life; To Take Refuge in the Three Treasures; Preach
According to the Capacity of Beings; The Bodhisattva

Chapter 7 Conclusion 116
Persons Revered in Japanese Buddhism; Bodhisattvas Revered in
Buddhist Temples; Buddhist Ethics; Art; Animals in Mahayana
Buddhism; What Mahayana Is Not; What It Means to be a
Mahayana Buddhist

Selected List of Books 124

Further Books on Mahayana Buddhism 125

A Short Glossary of Buddhist Terms 127

Appendix. Twelve Principles of Buddhism 129

Preface

It is assumed that the reader of this little book is already familiar with the life of the Buddha and the general ideas of his doctrine as they can be read in the manuals, both scholarly and popular, of Western writers. The life of the Indian prince who gave up his family and home to seek enlightenment, who obtained it under the Bodhi tree, and who then returned to the world to teach the Way to his fellow beings is well known. The doctrine of what is called Primitive Buddhism, but which is really a form of later Hinayana teaching, has also been explained by Western writers, as have the main points of this Buddhism, many of which are found in all forms of Buddhism. These main points are: The Three Marks of Impermanence (*anicca*), Suffering (*dukkha*), and Non-Ego (*anatta*); The Four Noble Truths: (1) The Existence of Suffering, (2) the Cause of Suffering, which is Desire, (3) the End of Suffering, and (4) the Way Out of Suffering, which is the Eightfold Noble Path; The Twelve-linked Chain of Causation; the Law of Cause and Effect, or Karma, and the teaching of perpetual flux, or becoming. This Buddhism holds up the ideal of Arhatship, the necessity for all men to strive after liberation from the wheel of birth and death.

Mahayana accepts many of these doctrines but holds some of them less important. What is most important in Mahayana is Enlightenment, freedom from Illusion, and the aspiration after Buddhahood, and this not only for a few wise monks but for all beings.

As this little book is on Mahayana Buddhism, I refer the reader to the many good books on early Buddhism, and, except for describing some of the chief differences to be found between Mahayana and Hinayana, will confine myself to the more important teachings of Mahayana Buddhism.

I have not in this Primer written anything about the Buddhism of Tibet. Much fine Mahayana teaching is to be found in Tibetan Buddhism, but it is so mixed with non-Buddhist elements that it

cannot be called pure Mahayana, which reveals itself in the teachings and documents of India, China, and Japan. Moreover, I am
not familiar enough with Tibetan Buddhism to feel myself com-
petent to write of it. In my own study, I have concentrated upon
Mahayana as found in India, China, and Japan, and most
especially in Japan, where I consider Mahayana Buddhism is
living most vitally today. Materials for this study are chiefly to
be found in books in the Japanese language by Japanese writers,
but I have consulted the works of prominent Western and Indian
scholars also.

Pali Buddhism was the first to come to the knowledge of
European scholars, and therefore of the general public. The books
and sutras of Mahayana came to their knowledge later, and
Mahayana is therefore not so well understood in the West (this
was written in 1938). Buddhists of the Southern School, and
others who are in sympathy with that form of Buddhism, may feel
that the development of Mahayana has taken it far away from
what they consider the early and true form of Buddhism, and
may even say that Mahayana is not Buddhism but a religion of
its own. Mahayanists reply that Hinayana is one aspect of Buddhism and Mahayana is another, and feel that their own religion
presents certain sides of the Buddhist teaching not to be found
in the Hinayana. Without always adhering to the letter of the
earlier teaching, much of which was monk-made in Hinayana
times rather than Buddha-made, they claim that they are preserv-
ing and maintaining the true spirit of the Buddha.

As Mahayana is the religion of the Buddhists of the North and
East of Asia it deserves to be studied and appreciated. Of late in
Europe there is a desire to know more of it, and as most of the
books on the subject are large and scholarly, the writer presents
this simple little book which, unpretentious though it is, yet aims
at giving readers the main points of Mahayana, in the hope that
thereby an interest will be created in the reader which will lead
to the study of the worthier and larger works.

I wish to thank my husband, Dr Daisatz Teitaro Suzuki, for
help and encouragement in the preparation of this book.

Kyoto, 1938   BEATRICE LANE SUZUKI

Introduction

1

There are several reasons or rather circumstances which led to the neglect of the study of Mahayana Buddhism by Western scholars. The principal of these is their prejudice against it, and their prejudice is partly psychological and partly historical. The West learned of Buddhism first from the Pali sources, and its students concluded that Pali Buddhism is genuine, and that whatever other forms of Buddhism there may be in the other parts of the world, they do not represent the teaching of the Buddha. The first information of any event generally leaves a very strong impression and offers an almost irrational resistance to later corrections. Historically, Pali Buddhism has found many able exponents in the West, and its texts either in the original Pali or in translations are accessible, whereas the canonical books of Mahayana Buddhism are written in Sanskrit, and their translations in Tibetan and Chinese are almost beyond the reach of ordinary students of Buddhism in the West.

Another reason why the Mahayana is indifferently treated by Western people is that it is not so stereotyped as Pali or Hinayana Buddhism. The latter has ceased to undergo any noticeable development since it left its original abode in India in the earlier stages of its history. There is enough scholasticism in it, and a very complicated system of analysis too. Its disciplinary measures are rigidly formulated. Hinayana Buddhism is more easily studied, and more easily practised if one wishes to do so. But the Mahayana prevailing in Tibet, China, and Japan presents an infinite variety of form; it is rich in imageries and symbols; its doctrines are quite contradictory, at least superficially; its philosophical background is hard to grasp; it seems to be inextricably bound up with all kinds of superstitions, either carried along from India or adopted in the new surroundings. In a word, the Mahayana being so mobile and adaptable and progressively-spirited, its form is difficult to take hold of. The Western mind, which has a strong craving for logic and system, is utterly bewildered when it faces the Mahayana. In this respect, H. C. Warren, the author of *Buddhism in Translations*, is right when he writes in his Introduction thus: 'After long bothering my head over Sanskrit, I found much more satisfaction when I took up the study of Pali. For Sanskrit literature is a chaos; Pali, a cosmos. In Sanskrit every fresh work or author seemed a new problem; and as trustworthy Hindu chronology and recorded history are almost nil, and as there are many systems of philosophy, orthodox as well as unorthodox, the necessary data for the solution of the problem were usually lacking.'

While the knowledge of Sanskrit and an acquaintance with the Sanskrit Buddhist literature in existence is needed in order to have an historical understanding of Mahayana Buddhism, the most essential thing in this connection is to be well informed on Chinese and Japanese Buddhism. The Mahayana sutras are written mostly in Sanskrit and partially in Prakrit, and Nagarjuna and Asanga and other Mahayana philosophers wrote many important commentaries on the sutras, and also developed in a logical manner some of the Mahayana thoughts. Nagarjuna was an acute dialectician, and his work on the Madhyamika or Middle Way is an able discourse on the subject. Asanga and his brother Vasubandhu were more psychologically minded, and the theory of the Alaya-vijnana (all-conserving soul) has paved the way to the systematisation of the Mahayana teachings concerning the Vijnanas (consciousness). We ought to know of all these philosophical attempts made in India. But unfortunately Buddhism is no longer alive in India. No doubt its spirit and some of its teachings have been absorbed by other Indian religions and philosophies. But Buddhism with all its religious aspirations and doctrinal differentiae is to be found only in China and Japan, for Buddhism is still a living spiritual and cultural force in these countries, and without the knowledge of this the Oriental peoples and their various activities, moral and political, are difficult to understand.

2

It was fortunate that the progressive nature and the ever-expanding missionary spirit of Mahayana Buddhism did not allow itself to be confined within the boundaries of its native land. While

Hinayana Buddhism moved towards the south, the Mahayana opened up a north-eastern course until it came over to Japan, where it is now, if we can say so, recruiting new forces to cross over the Pacific. If the Mahayana was to thrive in India, even after the successive rise of Nagarjuna and Asanga and other great Mahayanists, it had to follow two courses; the one along the philosophical route opened by them, and the other along that of extravagant symbolism whose inchoate movements were already noticeable in the Mahayana sutras themselves. Either course was sure to seal up for the Mahayana the further course of a healthy and profitable development, which actually took place. Neither the logical school of Nargarjuna nor the psychological school of Asanga and Vasubandhu made any further contribution to the thought-world of India; while the extravagantly luxurious imageries marshalled in such Mayhayana sutras as the *Vimalakirti*, the *Saddharma-pundarika*, the *Gandavyuha*, ended in the rise of the Vajrayana with which Buddhism lost its original significance.

When the Mahayana reached philosophically the stage of the Madhyamika school, its usefulness as a practical religion ceased. It had to be transplanted somewhere else; it required a new soil to grow afresh. When religiously it came to be matured in the *Gandavyuha* and other sutras, it was high time for it to rot if it were to continue its growth in the same climate. The Mahayana had to come to China to effect its rejuvenation or resuscitation.

The Chinese people stand in such a contrast to the Indians that they can be said to represent two poles. The former are pre-eminently practical, moral, and historically-minded, while the latter are altogether too metaphysical, transcendental, and above all worldly things. Their healthy combination alone saves the Mahayana from utter annihilation from the earth. Therefore I say that it was fortunate for the people of the entire world that the Mahayana was made to start its new life in China and Japan.

3

To ascertain definitely the character of the impact of Buddhist thought on the Chinese it is advisable to know what are the general trends of Chinese thought. As is well known, the Chinese are a practical people and their way of thinking is decidedly positivistic. They are strict observers of social convention; rules of propriety and decorum are rigidly imposed upon them. They are lovers of peace, though their history is full of wars – civil and foreign. They are industrious, and are bent on increasing their economic efficiency. Confucianism is their religion and philosophy. Confucianism was an incarnation of common sense and practical wisdom. There is in the teaching of Confucius no depth of thought, no flight of imagination, no soul-stirring religious emotion. He speaks of Heaven, but it is too far away from the everyday experiences of ordinary people. Heaven is the concern of the ruler and not of the ruled. The Way (*tao*) so-called is not necessarily heavenly, but rather earthly, for it means morality governing communal life. Confucius was idealised to a great extent, but it was he no doubt who struck the most vital point of Chinese psychology. When we know him, we know the Chinese.

It is true that we have Laotze, another great outstanding figure in the history of Chinese thought, whose existence can never be ignored when we wish to trace adequately the development of thought in the Far East. In some way Laotze can be said to have exercised just as much influence on Chinese culture as his rival, Confucius. But somehow we feel that Laotze's idea is not so thoroughly native to the Chinese as is that of Confucius. Some scholars think that Laotze derived his teaching from India. This cannot be historically proved, but it cannot be ignored either. He in all likelihood did not belong to the race or races who made up in his time the main part of Chinese culture growing up along the Yellow River. He might have come from the south-western part of China, where genial climate and possible contact with southern peoples nourished the Laotzean way of feeling and thinking. In contrast to the Confucian rigorism and conventionalism, Laotze is southern in his *laissez-faire* and happy-go-lucky attitude towards nature.

Confucianism however must be said to be quite characteristic of the Chinese mind, not only because it has been taken up by successive governments as their official moral and political code, but because even Taoism, which appears at first as exotic and anarchic, was transformed, once adopted by the Chinese people, into a form of legalism known as *Fa-chia*. The *Fa-chia* school emphasises the importance of laws in keeping society in order, and their strict observance is demanded of each member of it. Confucianism is prone to moral usage instead of its legalisation, but Taoism wants to have all kinds of tradition ignored which have any binding force, and yet on the other side it conceals the idea which promises to develop into legalism. In fact, Taoism has given birth to two lines of thought which apparently go against its own original tendency; the one is the *Fa-chia* and the other is the ultra-individualism of the *Yang-chih* philosophy.

The practical legalism of the *Fa-chia* as an offshoot of anarchical Taoism breathes the *li-fa* spirit of Confucianism. The *li-fa* means rules of propriety, and is no more than the standardisation of the moral or juridical spirit, which is no doubt an aspect of Chinese character.

4

It is not known exactly when Buddhism was introduced into China; such events are not generally subject to chronological treatment. What is most probable is that Buddhism came to China about the time of the Christian era, or perhaps even prior to it, along the trade route from the Gandhara district, over the Sung Ling range of mountains, and via the south-eastern quarters of the Shin-king province of China. This was at the beginning of the Latter Han Dynasty, or rather towards the end of the Former Han. As Buddhism began to spread in the Middle Kingdom, one of the first objections raised against it is noteworthy, as it most positively reflects the highly practical side of Chinese mentality. As far as its theoretical foundation was concerned, it had something that resembled Laotze's teaching. But the Buddhist practice went directly against the Chinese mode of feeling. The objection was that Buddhists did not work for their living. When they do not marry, they leave no issue, which means that their ancestral spirits are neglected and their line is discontinued. When they beg for food, they consume the earnings of other people who have to work extra hours to support idlers – which means the wasting of national wealth.

To the Chinese mind filial piety is the greatest thing on earth, and it partly consists in perpetuating the family line as long as possible, for thereby the ancestral spirits are cared for. The Buddhist celibate monks are living quite contrary to this idea, for which reason their life is not at all moral and is highly objectionable. As to not working for their livelihood, it may not matter very much while their number remains small, but when it grows larger it may become a problem to a certain extent. What I want here to note is the practical turn of the Chinese mind. The Chinese people love life most intensely; they do not take it so pessimistically as the Indians, they have no special desire to escape it. They of course hate as everybody else does all the pains and sufferings incidental to this worldly life, but they are always patient and bear them heroically. When the Buddhists came from India with their pessimism and world-negating asceticism, the Chinese did not mind their theory so much as their practice – a practice running counter to the idea of family-perpetuation and of working for one's livelihood.

This being so, Buddhism had to take into serious consideration the characteristic Chinese penchant for being practical, if Buddhism were to prosper in China and do good to the people. Of course, the Buddhist missionaries from Indian and Central Asia had no such premeditated scheme for their work, but, as the Chinese began to embrace Buddhism because of its superior appeal to their spiritual and philosophical needs, they had among themselves to effect an adjustment between their psychological peculiarities and the new religion. This steady unconscious effort finally bore fruit in the shape of Jodo (*ching-tu*) and Zen (*ch'an*).

5

In the meantime the Chinese people could not remain indifferent to the philosophy of the Mahayana. There was something in it reminding them of Taoism. Whether or no there is any historical relationship between the latter and Indian thought, the Buddhists were not slow to make use of the teaching of the Lao and Chwang school. This method of interpreting Buddhism was known as *ko-i*, 'expounding the sense'. The first contact naturally took place between the Sunyata idea of the *Prajnaparamita* and the Wu of Taoism. But it is a great question whether Sunyata was properly understood by the Chinese philosophers until the arrival of Kumarajiva and the rise of his disciples. Among the first

Mahayana texts translated into Chinese we find such sutras as the *Prajnaparamita, Vimalakirti, Nirvana, Pratyutpannasamadhi, Avatamsaka,* and so on. The production of these translations must have been an extraordinary effort on the part of those who were actually engaged in the work. This can readily be seen in the translations themselves. The thoughts and feelings expressed in the sutras were so entirely foreign to the Chinese mind that the translators must have exhausted their intellectual resources to find adequate expression for them. It took more than a few hundred years properly to assimilate them into the Chinese blood, especially when scholars were busily engaged in writing literary commentaries on the classical Confucian works which offer almost no parallel ideas to those of the Mahayana. They were no doubt thunderstruck when the Mahayanists declared all things to be empty or void, or that there were numberless worlds besides this earth, which were inhabited by Buddhas and Arhats and Bodhisattvas and non-human beings and many other fanciful creatures, or that if the Buddha wanted he could turn one second into a thousand kalpas and a thousand kalpas into one second, and that he could also make Mount Sumeru enter into one mustard seed without the mountain being crushed to pieces. The Laotzean followers were perhaps told that all things originated from nothingness (*wu*) but not that all things were Suchness itself or Emptiness itself. A long period of education was needed to be able to grasp the teaching of Mahayana Buddhism as expounded in its sutras. Naturally there were some extraordinarily gifted minds among the Chinese even as early as in the fourth century. The greatest figure, however, who made Mahayana thought really acceptable or digestible for the Chinese was Kumarajiva, who came to Chang-an in 401 when he was fifty-eight years of age. During the twelve years that followed, aided by his able disciples, he translated thirty-five sutras and shastras consisting of three hundred fascicles. Those translations were later criticised by Hsuan-chuang as not scholarly nor faithful enough to the original, but Kumarajiva knew better than the critic, though the latter was a native Chinese and Kumarajiva a foreigner from Northern India. Kumarajiva was surrounded by many capable native disciples and understood how to appeal to Chinese mentality; he aspired to present the sense in such a way and in such a style as to be readily understood by his readers. His translations were greatly admired by the non-Buddhist Chinese doctors, who were great stylists and rhetoricians. Even after Hsuan-chuang, who produced more literary and faithful translations, Kumarajiva's were not superseded by them. There are generally two schools of translators; the one is scholarly, and the other strives to reproduce the spirit. Hsuan-chuang belongs to the former and Kumarajiva to the second. Both are needed, as each does a useful work in his own field.

After Kumarajiva the great translator and expounder of the Mahayana was Paramartha (499–569) who came to South China in 546, arriving in Chien-k'ang, the capital of the Liang, in 548. He was unfortunate in many ways and had to wander about from place to place with no fixed abode and with no royal patrons. But in spite of his hardships and constant sufferings he was able to translate about eighty texts consisting of more than three hundred fascicles. He was a scholar of the *Mahâyana Samgraha Shastra* by Asanga and its commentary by Vasubandhu, which is an authoritative work on the Vijnanamatra school of India. Paramartha compiled his own notes on them, from which a special school started known as the Mahayana Samgraha. It was not however until Chi-i (538–97) and Chi-tsang (549–623) of the Sui dynasty that the native Chinese doctors of Mahayana Buddhism formulated their own views of the Mahayana, basing them on the sutras and shastras. The ground for this had been preparing for five centuries at least since the first introduction of Buddhism to China. Hitherto it was chiefly scholars from India who interpreted the doctrine for the Chinese. Of course there were many native followers who helped them to carry out their work to a successful end. But the latter did not take any initiative steps by themselves; they were not intellectually strong and matured enough to open up an independent course of study. Chi-i is the founder of the T'ien-tai (Tendai in Japanese) school, whose teaching is the development of the doctrine contained in the *Saddharmapundarika*, and Chi-tsang is the principal expounder of the shastras belonging to the Madhyamika school of India. His is known as the Sanlun school (Sanron in Japanese), as it has adopted the three treatises of the Madhyamika as the basis of its teaching. It is practically an extension of the Nagarjuna philosophy.

Chi-i was one of the greatest Chinese Buddhist philosophers.

Without him and Fa-tsang (643–712), the founder of the Avatamsaka school, Chinese Buddhism could not claim original contributions to the history of Buddhist thought. A religion is always kept alive by the successive rising of original thinkers and pre-eminently spiritual leaders among its followers. They push forward its movement and keep up its ever-enlivening power, however full of vicissitudes their history may be in the different countries where it is transplanted. Personalities are the life of a religion, and the value of a religion is judged by the personalities it will produce. And this is true in two senses: a religion must be backed by intellectually vital forces as well as by spiritual creativeness. A religion, however spiritually inspiring and ennobling, must be supported also by philosophy, while philosophy alone will never make up the vitality any religion may .exhibit. Prior to Chi-tsang of the San-lun school, Chi-i of the T'ien-tai, and Fa-tsang of the Avatamsaka, Mahayana Buddhism produced many pious spirits during the five hundred years of its activity among the Chinese people, and the time and soil were well prepared for the growth of those native intellects who were able to build up their own systems for the interpretation of the creative spiritual impulse at the back of their religion. Buddhism thus became really Chinese, at the same time bringing out many treasures which were not discoverable in India.

It is to be remembered that the spiritual vitality of Buddhism lies in its sutras and not in its shastras so-called, which are philosophical treatises, and this is what we naturally expect of religious literature. Whoever the compilers of the Mahayana sutras may be, they are genuine expressions of the deepest spiritual experiences gone through by humanity as typified in this case by Indian minds. Those experiences thus dressed in the Indian imagination and its tropical terminology were to be made Chinese and interpreted in accordance with the psychological peculiarities of the people. Chi-i's T'ien-tai system and Fa-tsang's Avatamsaka philosophy were thus their attempts to transform Indian Buddhism really into their own. Thereby Buddhism is now made to yield up its hidden stock. Chi-tsang's Madhyamika and Hsuan-chuang's Yogacara are fine works interpreting the ideas of the Indian masters for their countrymen, but by achieving this end they fulfilled their mission and there was no further development needed or possible for them. But Chi-i and Fa-tsang carried on their intellectual elaboration of the two greatest Buddhist sutras produced by the Indian religious genius: the *Saddharmapundarika* and the *Avatamsaka*. And just because of these sutras being worked upon and interpreted by the Chinese mind and not by the Indian, Buddhism has come to live in a new light, to display a new form of vitality unknown to India. This is the chief reason why in the study of Mahayana Buddhism the Chinese works are most essential. When the latter are adequately understood, the significance of Indian Buddhism or rather of Buddhism as a whole is grasped in its proper perspective.

As is later shown, when Chi-i and Fa-tsang, together with the practical appreciation by the Chinese and Japanese of the Mahayana, are understood, its message to the Far Eastern peoples and consequently to the world at large will be fully comprehended.

In order to see how the Chinese mind worked out its own Buddhist philosophy I will in the following pages give the barest outline of the Avatamsaka doctrine as propounded by Fa-tsang. It was in fact this school chiefly that influenced the thought of the Chinese scholars, Buddhist and Confucian, following Fa-tsang.

First of all, let me state that the signification of the *Avatamsaka* and its philosophy is unintelligible unless we once experience the state known as *abhishyanditakayacitta*; for otherwise the whole sutra becomes mere gibberish and nonsensical. *Abhishyandita* means 'dissolution', *kaya* 'the body', and *citta* 'mind'; that is to say, a state in which we are no more conscious of the distinction between mind and body. This may sound impossible, but in fact the distinction we make between mind and body is altogether conceptual and artificial, and this artificiality has a wonderful binding power over us. Because of this how hard we have to work to realise a state of dissolution, although it is the natural state in which we were born! *

This state of complete dissolution, where there is no more distinction between mind and body, subject and object, noesis and noema, is known as the realisation of absolute Sunyata ('Emptiness'), that is, Reality or Mind, to use Avatamsaka ter-

---

* For further information see Suzuki's *Essays in Zen Buddhism*, III, p. 123.

minology. Sitting at this centre, as it were, we look around and perceive that this is a world of *Hsiang-chi* and *Hsiang-ju*, 'interrelationship' and 'interpenetration', that is to say the Dharmadhatu; and it is vividly described by the Indian imagination in the *Avatamsaka* sutra and explained by Fa-tsang and his school.

Hsiang means 'mutual', *chi*, 'relation of identity', and *ju*, 'fusion' or 'penetration'. *Hsiang-chi* and *hsiang-ju* are the key ideas of the Kegon philosophy.* The *hsiang-chi* relation is spatial and static, while the *hsiang-ju* relation is temporal and dynamic. Spatially speaking, each individual object appears to be separate and independent and existing by itself. This is really an illusion, for things are intimately interrelated like a chain, and each one of its links contributes to the make-up of the chain. The very notion of a universe or cosmos suggests this fact. Without being orderly there will be no world, and an order means interrelationship. The Kegon scholars push the idea to its logical end, or rather they emphasise this aspect of experience in order to reach a systematic view of the world.

One of their favourite analogies to illustrate this state of interrelation and interpenetration is that of the Indra-jala, Indra's Net. This net, made of precious gems, hangs over Indra's palace. In each of these gems are found reflected all the other gems composing the net; therefore, when it is picked up, we see in it not only the entirety of the net but every one of the gems therein. In a similar manner, every object in this Dharmadhatu world is related to every other object and penetrated by it not only spatially but temporally. For this reason, every minute we live contains eternity. Eternal Now is our life; we do not have to seek eternity anywhere else but in ourselves. It is the same with the idea of space. The point I occupy is the centre of the universe, and it is in me and with me that it subsists. As a fact of pure experience, however, there is no space without time, no time without space; they are also interpenetrating, and in this sense there is no profanity, as may be charged by pious Christians when I declare myself to be God, in whom time and space lie dormant as before Creation. This was indeed the idea of the Buddha, who is reported at the time of his birth to have declared that 'I alone, above heaven and below heaven, am the honoured one'.

* Kegon (Japanese) = Avatamsaka (Sanskrit) = Fa-yen (Chinese).

One of Fa-tsang's teachings on Kegon or Avatamsaka is known as the doctrine of the Ten Mysteries, and this idea of *hsiang-chi* and *hsiang-ju* runs through it. One of the ten is the mystery of Mount Sumeru and a mustard seed. In the Mahayana sutras we often come across the statements that a mustard seed holds in it Mount Sumeru, that the 10-foot square room of Vimalakirti contains all the worlds with every one of their inhabitants and yet does not find it overflowing, nor do all the worlds feel cramped or inconvenienced. According to the Kegon philosophy, these mysteries are 'inexhaustible' (*akshaya*), and for this reason the vows of Samantabhadra are also inexhaustible – the vows to benefit and save the world with all its beings. That individual salvation is not the sole object of the Buddhist life is also explicable from the Kegon point of view.

8

The teaching however would not have made such profound impressions on the Chinese mind if it did not go in company with Zen. Zen developed in China along with the Buddhist mysticism of Sunyata, partly spurred by the Lao-chwang idea of 'doing-nothing-ness' (*wu-wei*), and partly in accommodation with the Confucian emphasis on practical life. Zen is not, as is maintained by Hu Shih, a revolt of the Chinese mind against Buddhism, but its assimilatory response to the latter, and by the Chinese mind we must mean the Confucian mind plus the Lao-chwangese mind. In Zen we truly find the efflorescence of this mind; otherwise how could it have influenced Chinese spiritual culture so unbrokenly ever since its maturity in the T'ang dynasty? It is true that Zen is not doing so very well these days in China, for China is at present at the cross-roads and puzzled where to direct her steps; but I am sure when she regains her equipoise she will know what to do with her Zen.

At all events we can say that Zen is the practical consummation of Buddhist thought in China and the Kegon (Avatamsaka) philosophy is its theoretical culmination. But, as I have stated elsewhere, in religion practical experience must go side by side with philosophy, and philosophy with experience. So in China the philosophy of Zen is Kegon and the teaching of Kegon bears its fruit in the life of Zen. It was only when this perfect mutuality or identification was affected that Buddhism began to start a new life in the Far East, shedding off its old Indian coat which proved to be no longer capable of keeping the inner spirit in healthy condition.

When I say Buddhism I mean Mahayana and not Hinayana. If it had been Hinayana which came to China and Japan, it is most problematical whether it could have undergone this rejuvenation. In all likelihood Chinese and Japanese Buddhism would be still in a state of hibernation. As to Japanese Buddhism, I will speak of it later. As far as Chinese Buddhism is concerned, it was the spirit of Buddhism as manifested in Mahayana and not in Hinayana that proved to be so spiritually and intellectually vital as to give great impetus to the Chinese mind. For this reason alone, the study of Mahayana is full of significance: in it we read the life of Buddha ever rejuvenating itself, and also its wholesome effect on the cultural life of a people among which it finds itself transplanted.

The T'ang was the golden age of Buddhist art and philosophy, and the Sung following it and stimulated by it reviewed its own thought, that is, the thought native to the Chinese soil. Politically, the Sung was constantly at war with the strong northern races, and the latter half of the period was filled with tragic events. But in the world of thought the Chinese mind was most active, reflecting the constant tension which characterised the entire period of the Sung dynasty. It produced a number of philosophers, poets, and artists, distinguishing the Sung from all the preceding periods. It was one of the most original and creative periods in the history of the Chinese people. It is a recognized fact that in all this Buddhism had a great deal to do. The strangest phenomenon is however that the great Confucian historians and philosophers almost vie with one another to minimise or altogether to ignore the part Buddhism as thought and institution played in the moulding of the Sung culture and philosophy. If they at all refer to Buddhist thought, it is to denounce it as not worth while studying or as of no use to the enhancement of moral life and teaching.

But with all their protests, denunciation, and indifference, they were deeply impressed in various ways by Buddhism and its followers. Their apparent indifference in reality spelt great concern, and by denying Buddhist thought they closely followed it. Their Unconscious decidedly betrayed their consciousness; it was really a psychoanalytical case of enantiadromia.

9

Roughly speaking, this was what the Mahayana achieved in China. The Buddhism that was destined to die away in India when left to its own resources was brought back to life in China and, more than that, it gave great stimulus to the Chinese mind and made it work out many things original to it. The Mahayana in India became in China on the one hand Zen, Kegon, and Tendai, and on the other hand Jodo (ching-tu), the doctrine of the Pure Land. If Zen appealed to the practical intellectual side of the Chinese mind, Jodo met its spiritual cravings. The desire to be born in a land of purity and happiness is the desire for immortality. Whatever form it may take with different individuals, they all have a certain longing for a life to come or a life to continue. Before Mahayana Buddhism came to China, the people did not have a very definite idea about their future; their religious horizon was very much limited to the earthly life or to an indefinite prolongation of it. The Chinese people have been pursuers from the beginning of their history of the three desires: Bliss, Prosperity, and Longevity. Bliss means perpetuation of the family life, while Prosperity and Longevity are, of course, matters concerning the individual. Buddhism did not oppose this outright, but taught the moral law of causation to attain this end. There is no doubt that this is one of the strong points Buddhism had made among the Chinese people, but it was no special merit which the Mahayana alone could achieve. Indeed, the idea is more emphatically upheld by the Hinayanists, as we see among the Southern Buddhists. What the Mahayana specifically achieved anywhere was just the opposite of this doctrine of moral causation. For its real doctrine of salvation is to transcend causality, in other words to make the transcendental power of Buddha work freely over the ignorance of all beings. This called forth the doctrine of the Nembutsu (*nien-fo* in Chinese and *Buddhanusmriti* in Sanskrit) as taught in such sutras as the *Sukhavativyuha* or the *Saptasatikaprajnapara-mita*.

The doctrine of Jodo or Pure Land developed early in China when Ye-on (Hui-yuan), 334–417, disciple of Do-an (Tao-an), established his retreat in Lo-han and founded the White Lotus Society. After him, there were a number of great Nembutsu followers, among whom one may mention Donran (T'an-luan, 476–542), Doshaku (Tao-ch'o, 562–645), Zendo (Shan-tao, 662), Hosho (Fachao, 768–821), and Jimin (Tz'u-min, 680–748). They all helped to develop the Jodo teaching in China, and at present it is in close association with Zen.

10

But it was in Japan that the Jodo reached its culmination by bringing the so-called 'other-power' wing of Mahayana Buddhism to its ultimate end. The one who thus matured the doctrine of the Pure Land was Shinran (1173–1262). He lived in the Kamakura era as a follower of Honen, who was the founder of the Jodo sect of Japan. The Kamakura marks in various senses a great epoch in Japanese history. For one thing this was a great age of religious revival and produced many great Buddhist souls whose spiritual influence is still felt among us of the twentieth century. Shinran may be said to be the foremost of these religious leaders or reformers. It was he indeed who first promulgated the doctrine of salvation by faith alone. According to him no work of merit was needed to bring a man or a woman under the grace of Amida, whose love of beings knew no bounds and imposed no condition whatever upon his devotees except absolute faith in him. However sinful a man or a woman might be, if he or she once pronounced his name in absolute sincerity of heart, it was enough to bring such a one at once into the most intimate connection with him; that is, salvation or a rebirth in the Pure Land was in a most definite manner assured. Is it not really wonderful to see that Buddhism, which started with the doctrine of self-salvation through enlightenment as it is still taught by the Hinayanists, has finally come to teach the doctrine of faith which alone has saving power for all sinners even with all their mountain-high load of sin on their shoulders! And Shinran, a Mahayanist, achieved this in

Japan after two thousand years' development of Buddhism in the Far East.

Some critics may say that Amidism is not Buddhism, and that if it is so anything can be Buddhism. But those who know know there is a logical, if it could be so termed, and necessary connection between Amidism and the Mahayana conception of Buddha as love and wisdom, as Mahakaruna and Mahaprajna. The readers of this manual will readily trace this connection step by step as they peruse it. Indeed, if not for Mahayana this form of spiritual development could never be effected. Hinayana is all right as far as it goes, and there are still many things in it which must be taken up by the Mahayanists for their most serious consideration. But if the Buddhism that came over to the Far East were Hinayana and not Mahayana, we could never have seen such a marvellous display of spiritual vitality as we have seen in China and Japan. Mahayana may yet perform wonders in years to come.

11

Some men then say this: If Mahayana is such a wonderful spiritual power as to be able to transform itself into anything, Amidism, Zenism, Ryobu-Shintoism, or Kobo's Shingon school, it has then nothing of its own, it is absolutely characterless, and it is the same as utter nothingness. This criticism is justifiable in a certain sense if 'nothingness' means inanity, mere negativeness, and death. But the strange fact is that out of the 'nothingness' of Mahayana all those spiritual phenomena rise and work their way variously into human minds and are vital enough to demonstrate their practical validity. Indeed Mahayana can be anything, and yet it always leaves its hallmark, proving that its creative sources are inexhaustible. If the time should come when Christianity and Buddhism or Mohammedanism and Buddhism are to be amalgamated into one form of religion, the approach or active advance would surely be made on the part of the Mahayanists, and not on the side of the other religions. There is indeed something in Mahayana that enables it to spread its ever-assimilative wings over all faiths and all thoughts.

Thus we can see that Mahayana Buddhism is not confined to the Buddhism of Nagarjuna and Asanga and other philosophers of

Indian Buddhism; it refers to a historical process still in forward movement which started in India from the creative genius of Sakyamuni Buddha more than two thousand years ago, and which, spreading itself north-eastward, reached China and Japan, and in these latter countries has produced several great schools of thought which are still in active movement and ready at any moment to shoot out something fresh and vital. This 'inexpressible' (*acinta*) and 'inexhaustible' (*akshaya*) Mahayana really deserves the serious study of the student of Oriental thought.

DAISETZ TEITARO SUZUKI

PART ONE

Chapter 1

Hinayana and Mahayana

1 CLAIM OF MAHAYANA

When the Buddha obtained Enlightenment under the Bodhi-tree two courses were open to him: one, to keep his knowledge to himself and to pass into the bliss of Nirvana; the other, prompted by compassion for other beings, to remain in the world to bestow the benefits of his wisdom upon all. These two ways mark the difference between Hinayana and Mahayana, for, while Hinayana does not by any means ignore compassion for others, nevertheless it stresses individual enlightenment. Mahayana, on the other hand, while not neglecting wisdom, nevertheless stresses compassion to such a marked degree that it overshadows the Hinayana in this aspect of Buddhism. As one writer* has remarked, 'The Mahayana stands firmly on two legs, Prajna and Karuna, transcendental idealism and all-embracing affection for all kinds of beings, animate as well as inanimate.' In Mahayana the attaining of wisdom is for the sake of the practice of compassion. What is one's own enlightenment worth, asks Mahayana, if it is not to help others to the same *summum bonum?* Individual enlightenment is not the goal of Mahayana so much as universal enlightenment.

Mahayanists claim that while Hinayana may provide the letter of the Buddha's teaching Mahayana has endeavoured to catch the true spirit of it. The difference, therefore, is a difference of interpretation.

When the Buddha died he said, 'I have not kept anything back.' This is made much of by many writers on Buddhism, who use it to assert that the Buddha had no esoteric doctrine. But Mahayanists believe not so much that he kept something back but that what he taught others did not find favour with the

* D. T. Suzuki, in *Outlines of Mahayana Buddhism.*

compilers of the Pali Canon (the sect of Vibhajjavadins), and so was left out. Further they claim that much of the Buddhist teaching was preserved by other disciples and written down in Sanskrit, later forming the Mahayana. Moreover, they consider that his teaching presents the true spirit of the Master's doctrine. As a modern Japanese scholar (Chizen Akanuma) remarks, 'The Mahayana movement is a movement of the revival of Sakyamuni's teaching which was about to die out as a result of the realistic teaching of Hinayana.'

2 EARLY HISTORY

There were Mahayanists at the time of the Buddha's death; that is, some of the 'hearers' were that way inclined, and interpreted Buddhism according to their own light.

Buddhism, which originated in the teaching of Sakyamuni, who appeared in India 2,500 years ago, may be divided into four parts.

1 Primitive Buddhism – the period from the beginning of the Buddha's teaching to 100 years after his Nirvana, 530–380 BC.
2 Hinayana Buddhism – the development of the different schools from 100 years after Buddha's death to AD 100.
3 Development of Mahayana Buddhism – Hinayana and Mahayana flourishing together. A new epoch in Buddhism, AD 106–300, Buddhism unified by Nagarjuna.
4 The predominance of the Mahayana, AD 300–500.

Buddhism was founded upon the ancient Indian religion and developed from it, its foundation stones being the Vedas, Brahmanas and Upanishads. It cannot therefore be conceived as something entirely separate, but should be regarded as a further growth of Indian religion. In the Buddha's time there was much confusion of thought and many teachers, but when the Buddha appeared, and became enlightened, he established his Middle Path, retaining what he thought good of the old teaching and rejecting the rest. Owing to the great personality of the Buddha, and the synthetic attitude of his philosophy, Buddhism soon became popular, and King Asoka in the third century BC strove to make it a world religion. Adapting itself to the thought of the time, it developed from Primitive Buddhism into the different Schools of Buddhism and then into Mahayana, thereafter becoming an even greater religion. Later, seeds of decay crept in and Buddhism came into conflict with Indian orthodox feeling. But what it lost eventually in India it gained to the south and north and east, and ultimately it influenced all Asian thought.

'Thus have I heard' – with this all sutras, Mahayana and Hinayana, begin, but it does not mean that 'I' have been a personal listener to the sermon given. Rather he is reciting what he believes to have been the Master's preaching. In this he is absolutely honest, but honesty and historical objectivity are not necessarily the same.

The first Council, supposed to have taken place soon after the decease of the Buddha, could not have left written records, that is, compiled literary documents of all the sermons delivered during his forty-nine years of activity as propagator of the Dharma. Such a Council could only record the general outlines of the Master's teaching, not in the form of formal sutras, but in sketches and short discourses such as we have in the *Sutta-Nipata*, the *Iti-Vuttaka*, the *Udana*, and elsewhere.

This being the case, the only way to trace the original teaching of the Buddha, unencumbered by commentaries, interpretations, and historical accretions, is to examine carefully and scientifically the literature of the Buddha's sermons and pick up the thread which runs through them. In this the Pali sources are not the only reliable guide, for the Chinese translations sometimes reflect earlier traditions, and point more faithfully to the primitive ideas which prevailed in the days of the Buddha. The Pali texts belong to a special school, and are to that extent inevitably biased. They are of the school of the Vibhajjavadins, and present for the most part a rationalistic theory of the Buddha's teaching. As A. Barriedale Keith remarks in his *Buddhist Philosophy*, p. 15, 'The pious respect attributed to the antiquity and authority of these texts by devout Buddhists is as natural as it is laudable. But it is strange to find that Western criticism, ruthless in probing the claims of its own sacred scriptures, has treated the Pali Canon with a respect so profound as to regard with open hostility any attempt to apply to these sources of information the same dispassionate scrutiny which

is demanded from the researcher into the history of Christianity.'
The Pali Canon was a gradual growth, and some of it is late.
Primitive Buddhism became transformed and crystallised by the
monks, and developed into what is known as Hinayana Buddhism.
It is therefore a mistake to take the Pali Canon used by present
Hinayanists as the direct teaching of the Buddha. Some modern
writers, notably Mrs Rhys Davids, are trying to show that these
Hinayana teachings are the product of cloistered monks, who have
distorted the true teaching of the Buddha, but this well-known
writer believes that these primitive teachings of the Buddha can
be recovered from the Pali books, and Mahayanists are certain
that they can be found in their own presentation of Buddhism.
As in most religions there is in Buddhism a conservative party, the
fundamentalists, and a broad-minded party, the modernists, the
Hinayanists representing the former and the Mahayanists the
latter. Six hundred years after the Buddha's Nirvana, Mahayana
sutras were rendered into Chinese, so they must have been known
in India long before the Hinayana sutras were completed. There
was so much rivalry between the two schools, however, that it was
natural that the Hinayanists should accuse the Mahayanists of not
having the authentic teaching of the Buddha, but Mahayanists
claim to have a direct line of inspiration.

The Buddhism which went to China was Mahayana; from
China it spread to Japan and has since developed through the
centuries in its own way. Whether historically authentic or not,
Mahayana has carried with it what it believes to be the true spirit
of the Buddha and has been the inspiration of millions of
followers.

Buddhism is a product of the fourth period of Indian thought,
and appeared at a time of conflict between the conservative and
the free-minded. It belongs to the non-Brahmanic side, and yet
includes the best thought that is in Brahmanism. Just as
Christianity changed from its primitive form to Pauline, and later
to Catholic, Protestant, and other interpretations of Christ's
teaching, so Buddhism changed from Primitive to Hinayana, and
from Hinayana to Mahayana, with many different schools within
each.

The original sects of Primitive Buddhism, the orthodox
Sthaviras and the progressive Mahasangikas, soon subdivided, and

became the sects of Hinayana, the Sthaviras resolving into eight and the Mahasangikas into ten. The most powerful of these sects and the one which lasted the longest was the Sarvastivadin (Japanese, Ubu). The Mahasangikas were the precursors of the Mahayanists, and the seeds of Mahayana can be found in the *Sutta Nikaya.*

The question arises: Was Mahayana really spoken and taught by the Buddha? The reasons given against it are:

1 That the Shaka of Mahayana is not an historical personage like the Shaka of Hinayana, but a super-human Buddha, specially created.
2 That the sutras of Mahayana did not appear until 600 years after the Buddha's death.
3 That Mahayana doctrine shows itself to be an addition to Hinayana's gradual development, and from this we can infer that the Mahayana scriptures were compiled by Ashvaghosa and Nagarjuna, and not directly taught by Sakyamuni himself.

Many scholars of the present day in Japan agree with this point of view, and it is taken by many Western scholars. On the other hand, among Japanese scholars and gradually appearing among Western scholars, for example in the works of the late Sir Charles Eliot, is the other opinion, that the doctrines of Mahayana or at least its seeds are to be found in Primitive Buddhism.

3 DEVELOPMENT OF MAHAYANA

The following are some of the most significant ideas which Buddha taught to his disciples. First, the nature of Dharma, which is the actual world we experience uninfluenced by the intellect (or Ignorance in Buddhist terminology), or by desire. It is that which persists when all intellectual systematisation and effective valuations are wiped away. When this process is not carried out to the last degree, misery clings to us, and there is no full emancipation. Metaphysical subtleties are useless, because they cannot grasp the Dharma as it is. Nor does moral asceticism, as practised by most religious leaders, release us thoroughly from the yoke of desire.

The Dharma is grasped when things are taken as they are, *yathabhutam*. It is therefore Tathata, Suchness or Thusness. One who has attained to this understanding is the Tathagata, 'one who has thus come', and it is only by this insight, known as Enlightenment, *bodhi*, that misery is conquered.

Misery arises from desiring things which are beyond one's reach. This world of multiplicities is a world of change, of constant becoming; it meets defeat, and defeat is pain. Desire presupposes an ego-soul, and this ego is the creator of a dualistic world. An ego proclaims itself by negating itself. The ego is now confronted with the non-ego, which is self-elimination. When so limited it awakens the desire to overcome its opponent, or rather to possess it. But this is self-contradiction, and cannot lead anywhere but to self-destruction. The ego hates to be destroyed, but its establishment is not achieved unless it commits suicide, and it dreads suicidal proceedings of any kind. Misery is the inevitable outcome.

Caught in this dilemma, the only course of escape is to find a higher standpoint where there is no dilemma. The Buddha's teaching thus becomes tinged with intellectuality, not in its ordinary dualistic sense but in the sense of transcendental wisdom (*prajna*).

The Twelvefold Chain of Causation is an attempt to explain this life of relativity, the clinging to which is misery. It is doubtful whether the Buddha taught this formula as it stands now, for the chain is not always twelvefold, being sometimes tenfold, sometimes fivefold, but he undoubtedly taught the mutual dependence of concepts, and his Enlightenment enabled him to transcend this state of dependence.

He found the way to a higher synthesis, not by following the course of ordinary logic but by intuitively experiencing the Dharma itself. His teaching of non-atman (*anatta*) is therefore not the outcome of intellect, but an intuition, a state of actual experience. It is useless to attempt to establish a theory of non-atman by means of analysis, as has been contantly done by Buddhist scholars since the days of Nagarjuna.

To realise this experience, the Buddha taught the Eightfold Noble Path, which includes the Threefold Discipline (*siksha*): morality (*vinaya*), meditation (*dhyana*), and transcendental wisdom (*prajna*). To train one's mind and body certain regulations are to be followed, and the Vinaya (moral discipline) is needed for this purpose. But this is not enough; a frame of mind conducive to the grasping of the Dharma, the truth of Suchness, must be cultivated. Dhyana is the discipline accepted universally by all the Indian philosophers, saints, and ascetics, and the Buddha had no reason to reject it. In fact, the practice of Dhyana constitutes one of the special features of Eastern moral culture. The value of transcendental wisdom, called Prajna, is not to be judged from the philosophical point of view, for it is a fundamental intuition and belongs to the deepest part of the soul. This threefold Discipline, when perfected, leads to emancipation, that is, Nirvana.

This is probably all that the Buddha taught his followers as the Middle Way. Any further elaboration must be regarded as containing ideas added by later commentators. The Hinayana school of Buddhism is therefore far from representing the Buddha's original teaching. It is a development as sound as is the Mahayana, only the latter is later than the former. A mass of Buddhist literature, known as the Abhidharma collection, contains much of the philosophical systematisation which was obviously added by later scholars, for we cannot imagine that such an intricacy of ideas was given by the Buddha to his followers. The same can be said of the sutra-class of Buddhist writings. They do not record the Buddha's sermons, but are more or less commentaries on them, written in this particular form.

In the so-called Hinayana school, the sutra-class of the canonical texts grew up along with that of the Abhidharma, and probably also with that of the Vinaya, but in the Mahayana the sutra-class came into existence first, and later such great minds as Nagarjuna, Asanga, Vasubandhu, and others appeared and prepared systematic presentations of the ideas expressed in the Mahayana sutras. The latter, therefore, are likely to have been compiled while the different schools of the Sthavira and the Mahasanghika were busily engaged in their own work of compilation.

The second great Council, alleged to have taken place in the reign of King Asoka, was the first occasion for serious schism, and took place between the Sthavira and the Mahasanghika. The Elders were naturally conservative, while the masses were liberal and inclined to give much freer interpretation to the Buddha's teaching. The latter were also disposed to study more seriously the question of Buddhahood, that is the study of Buddhology. The Elders were adherents to the letter of the scriptures, in the understanding of which they did not allow much latitude, but the masses wanted a thorough knowledge of the personality of the historical Buddha so that they could understand his teaching more intelligently. They wanted to find out what made the Buddha what he was, for, knowing this, they could more rationally and efficiently put his words into practice. The Buddha, they argued, must have been a most wonderful personality. If he had been no more than the author of the Hinayana sutras, the Abhidharma, and Pratimoksha, he might have been a great moral teacher, but he could not have exercised such a spiritual influence over not only his immediate disciples but those who followed. The reason that his 'words' were so inspiring must have been due to their being more than mere 'words'; there must have been something that moved them and made them a living power. The masses may not have consciously reasoned in this way, but something like this must have been operating in their minds. As a result, the Mahayana sutras were produced among the followers of the liberal school.

It is extremely hazardous to put anything approaching a chronological order to the sutras known as Mahayanist, but one can safely state that the Prajnaparamita group belongs to the earliest period of Mahayanist activities, and was probably produced in the first century BC. It is therefore possible that while the Agama or Nikaya group of sutras was being written among the Hinayana followers, the *Prajnaparamita* was being prepared, though in a more primitive form than that in which we now have it. It is equally likely that the *Sukhavativyuha Sutra* already existed, though also in a cruder form.

If we fix the date of Nagarjuna as the early part of the first century AD, those sutras mentioned in his works must have already existed, and assumed an authoritative nature for the Mahayana followers. As said before, the Mahayana first appeared in sutra form, and did not enter into philosophical discussion until its ideas were formulated by Nagarjuna. This was natural, because the Mahayana is above all the expression of religious aspirations, and has no inclination to indulge in speculation. Of the sutras thus produced prior to Nagarjuna we may mention the following: *the Prajnaparamita, the Saddharma-pundarika, the Dasabhumiaka, the Gandavyuha, the Vimalakirti,* and *the Sukhavativyuha.*

At first sight the Mahayana may appear uncouth, unwieldy, and bewildering, but when one grasps some of its leading ideas its sutras are not so incomprehensible as they at first appear. Western students of Buddhism must remember that their first acquaintance with Buddhism was the Pali texts, belonging to a school of the Sarvastivadin which historically stands to a great extent in opposition to the Mahayana. Where the Sarvastivadin is inclined to accept the world in its dualistic expression, the Mahayana goes further into the very reason that makes its existence possible, and this not in the fashion of the philospher but as an earnest seeker of ultimate truth, as one who aspires to come in direct contact with Reality itself. Intuition, therefore, more than analytical speculation, is valued in the Mahayana. To induce this frame of mind it introduces its followers to a series of negations. As shown in the *Diamond Sutra,* every proposition of logic is in turn denied, which is a staggering idea, but until we are thus thoroughly cleansed of all the intellectual habits contracted since our birth we cannot expect to see the Dharma itself. It is then alone that the Dharma reveals itself, as God reveals himself to a thoroughly repenting soul.

Buddhology plays a large part in the Mahayana, for Mahayanists held that by getting in touch with that which really constitutes the being of the Buddha, they could the better apply his teaching in their daily life. They realised that they might not be able to be like the Buddha in every respect, but when they could see at least the direction of the Buddhahood there was a great gain in their spiritual life. Their interest in the Buddha himself thus equalled that in his various teachings. They were impressed by the fact that the Buddha was 'the Enlightened One', and that Enlightenment (*bodhi*) came to him after many years of the higher moral life (*paramita*). While he was thus perfecting himself he was a Bodhisattva, 'one who seeks Enlightenment'. Here, then, was the significance of the Jataka tales with the Mahayanists as well as with the Hinayanists, but the conception of Bodhisattvahood reached fuller development with the Mahayanists. The object of the Buddhist life in their view was not Arhatship but Bodhisattva-hood; when this was attained, Buddhahood would be more readily realised. Bodhi, Bodhicitta, Bodhisattva, Paramita – these are the words most frequently met with in Mahayana literature. When these are established the notion of vow (*pranidhana*) is inevitable. The Buddha is now no longer historical; he is the object of religious aspirations, he is eternal.

When the Buddha ceases to be historical, in the sense that he is no more subject to the so-called laws of nature, he is what is technically known as in Sambhogakaya, the Body of Enjoyment, and whatever sermons he gives in the Mahayana sutras are given in this capacity. The world he sees, the events taking place in connection with his appearance and the language he uses are all radiations from his Sambhogakaya. We are thus no more in this world of relativity but are in a mysterious way transferred to another world under the suzerainty of a transcendental being.

The Mahayanists conceive this supernaturalness as an expression of Mahakaruna in the mind of the Bodhisattva. Mahakaruna is not mere *karuna*, love, or sympathy, or compassion, as ordinarily understood; it is a great love not to be experienced by those possessed of the idea of self. For 'great' read 'transcendental' or 'absolute', the love which is the basis of all other forms of love. It is this great love which moves the Buddha out of his meditation to bring salvation to the world.

The Buddha by his transcendental wisdom sees all things from their inception to their final disappearance; his eye surveys everything to its destiny; his all-knowledge perceives *karma* as it works out its teleology. In other words, he watches all things from the point of view of *Sunyata*. This is a very difficult term to translate. When it is rendered 'emptiness,' 'vacuity,' or 'nothingness', it is subject to gross misunderstanding. It will be explained later; let it suffice here to mention that it does not mean anything negative, the deprivation of all positive thoughts whereby a bare blankness of things is left. Sunyata is what is left behind after an endless series of negations, and is therefore the most positive and fundamental of ideas.

When these fundamental ideas of the Mahayana are grasped, all that seemed utterly bewildering becomes transparent, and all the apparently supernatural wonders described in the Mahayana sutras, together with their abstruse or 'absurd' contradictions, glow with a significance never dreamed of before.

4 FURTHER CONSIDERATIONS OF HINAYANA AND MAHAYANA

The word Hinayana was an invention of the Mahayanists, and means the small vehicle. The present Hinayanists call their school the Theravada, 'Doctrine of the Elders', yet, as we have seen, there is a question as to what constitutes the Theravada, for if Primitive Buddhism is the Theravada then surely the Hinayanists are as far from it as the Mahayanists.

In early times the life of the mendicant monk was considered the highest. To become a good disciple and to attain liberation for oneself was the goal, whereas with the Mahayanists it is to become a Buddha and save others.

With the Mahayanists four points were prominent: First, they were progressive and affirmative. Secondly, whereas the Hinayanists developed with the Order as the centre, the Mahayanists concentrated rather upon the individual, so that at first there were no schools among them but rather individual teachers, such as Nagarjuna and Asanga, and although schools developed later in Mahayana they were still centred upon individuals. Thirdly, while the Hinayanists laid the greatest stress upon the Tripitaka, the Mahayana was content to propagate the Buddha's fundamental teaching wherever found. Compared with them the Hinayanists were both formal and systematic in their scholastic orthodoxy. A fourth and the most outstanding point was that whereas Hinayana was a forest or mendicant renunciative way, Mahayana, while not excluding this feature, wished to make the Buddhist life open to all, priest and layman alike. With it the ideal became not the Arhat bent upon his own salvation but the Bodhisattva to which all may aspire. This was and remains the most important of many important points in Mahayana.

With regard to doctrine there are five important differences to be observed. First as to the Buddha. In Hinayana he is a man like us, though the Mahasangikas, the progressive school, viewed him as eternal and ideal infinite power. In Mahayana the Buddha is indeed transcendental, eternal and absolute, and as such he saves all beings by the use of his Three Bodies (*trikaya*), a doctrine which we will consider later in more detail.

Another great point in Mahayana doctrine is the idea of the Bodhisattva. In Hinayana, there is but one Bodhisattva, the former birth of Sakyamuni, but in Mahayana an infinite number of Bodhisattvas are found. The Bodhisattva takes a vow to attain perfect knowledge and to save all sentient beings.

The world view of Mahayana is a third point to be noted. According to Mahayana there is a great principle which flows under everything; this gives rise to the *Alayavijnana* doctrine which constitutes the world view of Mahayana, in which everything centres upon the idea of the One Mind. Thus Mahayana idealism is contrasted with Hinayana realism. Fourthly, there is the doctrine of Sunyata, 'All things are empty'; but this does not mean that all is negation, but that all things are manifestations. The supreme reality in this world of relativity is the law of change, but in the world of Nirvana it is Emptiness, which is above all relativity. In Hinayana, suffering is something to be escaped from, but in Mahayana there is developed the idea that in suffering there is meaning, that it is indeed the very principle of religion and makes a way to deliverance. To transcend this world of suffering is deliverance which turns causation into Emptiness (not nothingness), thus getting rid of relativity, which is to destroy the individual world of selfishness, which in turn reveals a new world – the world of Reality. The Bodhisattva voluntarily and joyfully accepts pain if he is able thereby to help others, and he would never wish to attain his own salvation until all other beings are emancipated. As Vimalakirti says, 'As all other beings are sick, so I am sick.' All beings are considered one.

Finally, in Hinayana Nirvana tended to be negative, and the way of practice to attain it was largely negative. Not to do evil was more emphasised than to do good, whereas Mahayana with its Bodhisattva ideal considered the active method as superior. While Hinayana, therefore, emphasises the Four Noble Truths and the Eightfold Noble Way, the Mahayana turns to the Paramitas for its way of practice. Nirvana in Hinayana is a tranquil state of separation from transmigration, but in Mahayana this very state is Nirvana itself. To understand the meaning of true Emptiness is to experience Nirvana.

These are some of the main differences between Mahayana and Hinayana. It is mainly a difference of outlook. Mahayanists do not look down upon Hinayana teachings, as is sometimes asserted, but consider that Hinayana is good as far as it goes and for some minds. They think that their own teachings go further and rise higher, and are for those who feel that the Buddhist teaching in Hinayana is too negative and self-centred, and who wish for the more positive, active and all-embracing unity, which they believe to preserve the real spirit of the Buddha's life and teaching.

To sum up, the main differences between the Hinayana and Mahayana are:

1 The interpretation of Buddhahood. In Hinayana, it is historical and ethical; in Mahayana, meta-physical and religious.
2 The conception of non-ego. In Hinayana it is analytical and scholastic; in Mahayana it is experiential and intuitive.
3 The altruistic point of view of salvation of the Mahayanists compares with the individualistic view of the Hinayanists.
4 The lessening of distinction between monk and layman in the Mahayana.
5 The comparative conception of Nirvana.
6 In the Mahayana all may attain to Buddhahood, for all have the Buddha-nature (Buddhata) and the desire for Bodhi.
7 The Bodhisattva and Arhat ideals.

Germs of Mahayana, however, are found both in Mahasanghika and Sarvastivadin. At the ancient Indian university of Nalanda all three points of view were taught. The Mahasanghikas contributed the idea of the eternal Buddha and the germ of Bodhisattvahood, the Sarvastivadins the Kaya conception in a rudimentary form. In fact, even before Mahayana had developed as such there were present in the Hinayana its principal ideas. As the late Sir Charles Eliot said: 'These ideas (of Mahayana) are all to be found in the Nikayas, sometimes as mere seeds, sometimes as well-grown plants. But between early Buddhism and the Mahayana there is a great difference in emphasis.'

Among the points of view which are the same in Hinayana and Mahayana are the following:

1 The object of Buddhism is to get rid of delusion, obtain enlightenment, and enter the world of the Infinite and Absolute.
2 The world has no beginning and no end. All is explained by causation, but there is no first cause.
3 All things change, all is impermanent, all is transient. This is true not only of men but of all life, even that which seems most enduring.
4 There is no substantial entity known as the 'Ego'. As all is impermanent and transient, so there is no self or ego such as is popularly regarded as persisting behind consciousness.
5 The law of causation is universally valid in the moral world as well as in the physical world. Every cause has an effect.
6 Transmigration explains causation, and is due to karma, and karma is produced by the deeds in the life of birth and death. Transmigration leads to suffering, as the Four Noble Truths set out.
7 Delusion is the cause of suffering which is universal.
8 Moral practices, such as the Eightfold Noble Path and the Paramitas, are prescribed in order to remove delusion.

In regard to the nature of Nirvana we shall find that Mahayana and Hinayana differ, but they are both firm in the belief that Nirvana is attainable, by means of Arhatship and Bodhisattvaship respectively.

Mahayana means 'great vehicle', in contrast to Hinayana's 'small vehicle'. The idea is that the Mahayana carriage or vehicle is large enough to carry all beings to salvation, while the small carriage of Hinayana can only carry the few. Mahayana absorbs Hinayana into itself, but Hinayana, or, as it calls itself, the Theravada (which term however must not be confused with the earliest Buddhist teaching), does not accept the Mahayana.

Mahayana is thought by some to have been founded by the great scholar Nagarjuna, but, as we see, he was a great systematiser and expounder of Mahayana rather than its founder, because in his works or translations and commentaries he mentions

Mahayana sutras already existing. Mahayana in reality was the outcome of the Buddha's thought, the germ of which can be found even in the Pali canon as preserved in certain circles, especially among the Mahasanghikas, and developed by them to a point at which they could easily pass to further development under the guidance of such men as Nagarjuna, who was a sage of extraordinary wisdom and insight. One of the Mahasanghika ideas which passed into Mahayana is the conception of the Buddha himself. In their Buddhology the idea of the Trikaya or three bodies of the Buddha is already latent, to be developed in the Mahayana. The idea of the Buddha-nature in all and its flowering in Enlightenment is also hinted at by the Mahasanghikas, and it is they who coined the word Bodhisattva-yana, which soon became Maha-yana.

The kernel of Mahayana is Deliverance for all, for all stand in relationship, which is causation, and Mind is the origin of all causation. Yet Mind, Buddha, and Beings are one. The real object of Mahayana Buddhism is to obtain enlightenment, to get rid of delusion, and to benefit others without hope of reward.

But are we not losing ourselves in a forest of brambles when we spend so much time over the problem of the historicity of Hinayana or Mahayana? Why not accept both as representations of the same truths, and take that one to ourselves which is best suited to our own minds?

Chapter 2

1 CAUSATION, KARMA, NON-EGO

Mahayana, like Hinayana and Primitive Buddhism, accepts the three fundamental principles: 1 All is transitory, 2 All is suffering, 3 All is egoless; and, based upon these, are the so-called Four Noble Truths: 1 All existence is suffering, 2 Suffering is caused by desire, 3 The extinction of desire leads to extinction of suffering, and 4 The way to the extinction of suffering is the Eightfold Noble Path, the steps of which are Right Views, Right Aspiration, Right Speech, Right Behaviour, Right Livelihood, Right Effort, Right Mindfulness and Right Concentration.

Suffering results from rebirth, which is due to Karma working according to the law of cause and effect. Karma controls the universe as well as individuals, and is due to ignorance, *avidya*, which involves a series of rebirths. The doctrine of ignorance is expressed in the following formula of the Twelve Nidanas or Causal Chain.

(1) In the beginning there is Ignorance (*avidya*); (2) from Ignorance comes Action (*sanskara*); (3) from Action comes Consciousness (*vijnana*); (4) from Consciousness, Name-and-Form (*namarupa*); (5) from Name-and-Form, the Six Organs (*sadayatana*); (6) from the Six Organs, Touch (*sparca*); (7) from Touch, Sensation (*vadana*); (8) from Sensation, Desire (*trishna*); (9) from Desire, Clinging (*upadana*); (10) from Clinging, Being (*bhava*); (11) from Being, Birth (*jati*); and (12) from Birth comes Pain (*dukkha*).

Vasubandhu explains it thus. According to his *Abhidharmakosa*, the formula runs: 'Being ignorant in our previous life as to the significance of our existence, we let loose our desires and act wantonly. Owing to this karma, we are destined in the present life to be endowed with consciousness (*vijnana*), name-and-form (*namarupa*), the six organs of sense (*sadayatana*) and sensation (*vedana*). By the exercise of these faculties we now desire for, hanker after, cling to these illusive existences which have no ultimate reality whatever. In consequence of this 'Will to Live' we potentially accumulate or make up the karma that will lead us to further metempsychosis of birth and death.'

From the problem of ignorance we come to consider non-atman or non-ego. This doctrine of non-ego is difficult to understand, and different interpretations of it are given by different Buddhist writers. It simply means that beings and things have no ego entirely of their own. To have any true individuality they must be united in the Dharmakaya. This will take place through enlightenment, when the true meaning of non-ego will be revealed. It means the elimination of selfishness, for there is only one true self, the Dharmakaya, and there can be no sense of separateness from it. But what the True Self is can only be found out through the experience of enlightenment. Anything predicated of it is only theory and a maze of words, and while many books have been engaged in discussing it the wise Mahayanist leaves it to intuition to disclose it.*

2 THE BUDDHIST DOCTRINE OF KNOWLEDGE

There are, according to Mahayana thinkers, different forms of knowledge. According to the Yogacara School of Asanga and Vasubandhu there are three forms, Illusive (*parikalpita*), Relative (*paratantra*), and Perfect or Absolute (*parinishpanna*). According to the Madhyamika School of Nagarjuna, there are two; Conditional or Relative Truth (*Samvritti-satya*) and Transcendental or Absolute Truth (*Paramarthasatya*). It is the object of all Buddhist teaching to lead beings to Absolute Knowledge (*prajna*).

We shall consider first the three forms. Buddhism lays much stress upon illusion, and teaches that many of the troubles of life are due to their illusory aspect, because the idea of egoism belongs

* All these points of Buddhist teaching will not be here explained in detail, as this has been done in many books on Buddhism, with some of which the reader is doubtless already familiar. Moreover in Mahayana they are not so much talked about as simply taken for granted to clear the way for further conceptions, such as enlightenment and salvation.

to this form and promotes all ignorant beliefs and practices, religious and otherwise. A favourite example given by the Mahayanists is the analogy of a rope and a snake. We are deceived by the similarity between them and often take the rope for a snake. Without inquiring further as to the real existence of the snake, we frequently assume it to be real and act accordingly, thinking that everything is in reality what it seems to be.

The second form of knowledge is relative, sometimes spoken of as accommodated truth, which asserts that we cannot know absolute truth in our practical everyday life, and therefore that relative truth is sufficient for the field of human experience. It is conditional, empirical, pragmatic, and serves for ordinary life. Most philosophical and religious teachings belong to this category, religion being accommodated to our ability of mind. Buddhism believes that even such of its own doctrines as are not the result of direct spiritual experience belong to this form of knowledge, the doctrines, scriptures and ceremonies of all religions, including its own, being regarded as relative or accommodated. For this form of knowledge the Japanese use the word *hoben* ('expediency', or 'device') which is the accommodated truth for the benefit of the unenlightened.

As relative knowledge is for the unenlightened, absolute knowledge is for the enlightened. It is a matter of experience, and efforts to explain it belong to the realm of relativity. It is the perfect or absolute knowledge or enlightenment which leads to ultimate salvation or Nirvana.

To continue the analogy of a rope and a snake; an unenlightened man walks over something long and thin in the moonlight and, taking it for a snake, is terribly frightened. This is illusion. For when he examines it more carefully he finds it to be a piece of rope. Ordinarily we go no further, being satisfied with this relative knowledge. But the rope is made of straw, its existence is dependent on that; it is not an absolute entity, and there is no finality in it. Therefore, it is not real knowledge, and no enlightenment comes out of it. Unless we go beyond the realm of relativity, and experience what lies behind the world of the rope, or that which makes the existence of the universe possible, no true salvation is possible.

This, however, does not mean that rope, as rope, has no use

in our practical life. Relative knowledge has its value as long as our relative existence continues. The mistake only arises when we take relative knowledge for absolute knowledge. The point is to use the rope for tying up bundles, but not for crossing the stream of birth and death.

The Madhyamika School instead of three forms of knowledge proclaims two kinds of truth, Relative or Conditional Truth (*Samvritti-satya*) and Transcendental or Absolute Truth (*Paramarthasatya*). Here the terms 'truth' and 'knowledge' are interchangeably used, and Nagarjuna's relative truth includes the illusion and relative knowledge of the former school of thought.

Relative truth concerns the conditions of this phenomenal world, which have to be taken as real for practical purposes, but we must know absolute truth if we want to see things as they really are.

Nagarjuna asserts that those who do not know the distinction between the two truths do not understand the meaning of Buddhism. The Madhyamika calls the highest truth 'Void' (*sunya*), in that nothing connected with relativity can be predicated of it, but Void does not mean nothingness; it is only void or empty of all relative terms and descriptions. In other words, it is absolute; that is, all that can be said of it fails to give any correct idea of it. In fact it is no idea at all, as it is to be intuitively grasped and not logically represented. The intuitive understanding of Void constitutes Enlightenment.

3 TATHATA, NIRVANA

1 THE MAHAYANA DOCTRINE OF TATHATA (SUCHNESS)

Absolute knowledge constituting Enlightenment is the knowledge of the Absolute which is absolute truth. In Buddhist terminology it is the knowledge of Suchness (*Tathata* in Sanskrit and *Shinnyo* in Japanese). 'Suchness' may sound strange to the Western mind, but Buddhists think it most expressive. What is Suchness? It is to see things as they are in themselves, to understand them in their state of self-nature, to accept them as themselves. This seems easy, for when we see a flower before us we know it is a flower and not an ink-stand or a lamp, but our knowledge is always coloured with all kinds of feelings, desires, and imaginations, and no such knowledge is pure and free from subjective 'defilements'. Mahayanists go even further and declare that this knowledge itself is the outcome of the self-asserting subjectivity of the knowing mind. To the Buddha's mind the flower is the inkstand and the inkstand is the lamp.

To see things as they are, that is to say in this state of suchness, means to go back to a state of mind before the division of the knowing and the known takes place. The dividing mind is the result of discrimination, and discrimination is going to the other end of suchness, which is grasped only when no discrimination takes place. The knowledge of suchness is therefore the knowledge of non-discrimination. When we discriminate, a world of dualities ensues, and this polarisation clouds the mirror of Prajna. Finally, the Dharma or Reality is lost sight of and the mind is 'defiled'. The Dharma is to see things as they are, in a state of *Yathabhutam*, which is another word for suchness.

The *Prajnaparamita Sutras* are the earliest works of the Mahayana school in India, in which most of the major ideas of the school are expounded. In these sutras the Buddha is often referred to as the Tathagata (*tatha + agata* or *tatha + gata*), which means 'one who thus comes or goes'. Whether he is the one who is come or gone does not concern us here, for the question is about the term 'thus' or 'such' – *tatha*. What makes up the essence of the Tathagata is this suchness, for without it he is not such as he is; that is, he is no more Tathagata. But this suchness does not belong to him only; it is possessed by all his followers, in fact by all beings, and it is something that neither comes nor passes away; nor is it subject to destruction, nor to obstruction, nor to discrimination. As long as all beings hold it within themselves they partake in the suchness of the Tathagata, that is to say they are neither born nor dead. In this the Tathagata and all beings are one and not two. When we talk about all beings being born we imagine that they follow the way of matter or mind, but the truth is that such things are born and pass away in the suchness of the Tathagata, while this suchness remains itself through the past, present and future. When, however, reference is made to the oneness of suchness in the Tathagata and all beings, we must not picture this suchness as existing by itself, as something separate from all beings, as enjoying its own existence as suchness, for 'Suchness to be regarded as suchness is no suchness', says the author or compiler of the *Prajnaparamita Sutras*.

From this one can see that by the suchness of the Tathagata is meant his Truth, his Reality, whereby he is what he is. When suchness means 'being so' it is Truth; when it suggests an idea of substance or self-nature it is Reality, and is sometimes found with *bhuta* prefixed. *Bhuta-tathata* may, however, be taken to mean being 'truly such'.

Our ordinary knowledge is never able to take hold of suchness, for its nature is to discriminate, to divide, to dwell on dualities, and suchness is just on the other side of it. The suchness of the Tathagata is the suchness of all beings, and these suchnesses are one and not two, says the *Prajnaparamita*, but at the same time suchness is no more suchness when it is so designated and regarded as something separate, existing by itself as the One, because in this case suchness is discriminated, and thereby becomes an object of ordinary knowledge. We cannot, therefore, form a picture of suchness in the way that we conjure up an image of an atom as something infinitely small, like a grain of sand in the Ganges. Suchness is not in the world of the senses, nor is it an idea created by logical conventions. It is something unthinkable, unrepresentable, unnameable, indescribable. For this reason, when the *Prajnaparamita* begins to talk about it, it is full of contradictions and negations.

2 SUNYATA AND PRAJNA

Suchness thus seems to be the most appropriate term to point to the presence of something in our experience with the world whereby all ordinary knowledge finds its validity. The Mahayanists were not, however, fully satisfied with the term, for they wanted to incorporate it in the system of thought to be traced back to the mind of the Buddha himself. They therefore called it Void (*sunyata*). *Sunyata* is thus *tathata* and *tathata* is *sunyata*. Void is suchness and suchness is void. The term 'void' has been in use in Buddhism since the beginning of its history, but its meaning had not been defined beyond its being identified with nothingness or emptiness, in the sense of absence of content. The Mahayanists made it mean the same thing as suchness.

It is the most daring declaration to state that all particular objects which we see about us, including ourselves, are void, of Void, from Void, with Void, and in Void. They stand in every possible prepositional relationship to Void. When Void is understood in the sense of emptiness and made to stand in contrast to fulness or substantiality the gravest fault is committed. Against this the Mahayanists had constantly to fight, because our ordinary way of thinking is to divide, to polarise, to set one thing or idea against another. It is the most unfortunate event in our life of thought that we have inherited a stock of language with the meanings given to it by our ancestors, and that when we have a new idea which was never thought of by the latter we have 'to fill the old bottles with new wine'. It is for this reason extremely difficult to make Western readers realise what void means in its Buddhist sense, for they have never come across this way of seeing things in their history of thought. So let us repeat once more that Void is not to be confused with nothingness, contentlessness, mere negation of existence.

The Mahayanists assert that Void is not an object of intellection but of Prajna, that is, it is to be understood intuitively. There is no use arguing about it; the point is whether you have it or not. If you have it not, no amount of argument, no array of reasonings will convince you of it. Once Prajna is awakened, however, you will know instantly what Void is, and, however logical and unassailable the philosopher's dialectical march may be, you will never be dispossessed of what you have taken hold of. This is the meaning of the following phrases so frequently met with in the Mahayana Sutras: 'Do not think of exercising Prajna, nor think of not exercising Prajna, nor think of doing anything with Prajna in any possible way you can think about it; for then you will not be exercising Prajna.' The *Prajnaparamita* thus concludes that Prajna is the mother of all Buddhas and that Prajna is all-knowledge. This latter statement means that Prajna is the source of all knowledge, that knowledge ordinarily so called is born of Prajna, though Prajna itself is not the object of knowledge.

Here we notice two aspects of Prajna: Prajna in itself and Prajna in its relation to knowledge. In a similar manner, the Mahayana speaks of Suchness as having two aspects. It will be better to say that our intellect compels us to put this qualification on suchness or void. The first is unchangeable suchness or void in itself, and the second is conditionable suchness or no-Void. The following quotations from the *Awakening of Faith*, traditionally ascribed to Asvaghosha, will clarify the points so far made about the Mahayana conception of Suchness. Asvaghosha, from his psychological point of view, has Mind for what is designated here as unchangeable suchness, and speaks of the Mind as suchness and the mind as birth-and-death, which corresponds to conditionable suchness.

'The Mind as Suchness means that the world of multitudes in its general all-inclusive aspect is one, and that the Mind as such is the principle of order which keeps things regulated. The Mind is essentially not subject to birth and death. All objects infinitely diversified come to be distinguished only because of our wrong ways of thinking. When freed from them, the world in its multitudinousness disappears. All things, therefore (which appear so varied to our minds) are primarily beyond the realm of discursive understanding, name-ability, or comprehensibility; they are intimately of sameness, suffer no transformation; they are not subject to destructibility. They are of the One Mind, and therefore to be designated as suchness. . . .'

Asvaghosha now goes on to describe more fully the nature of Suchness. 'As far as Suchness itself is concerned, it is the same in all beings, it knows no increase in the Buddha and Bodhisattvas, and no decrease in other beings; it was not born in the past, it will not pass away in the future; it remains constant and unchanged. From the first it contains in itself all virtues and there is nothing wanting in it. That is to say, it has in itself the great light of Prajna whereby the entire universe is illumined to its furthest end; it has the knowledge of Truth; it is the mind retaining its original purity; it is eternal, blissful, self-ruling, and free from defilement; it is cool and refreshing, unchanged and unfettered. It thus fulfils all the Buddha-virtues, surpassing in number the sands of the Ganga, and these virtues are not separable (from Suchness itself). They are with it, uninterrupted by it, they are united to it, they are beyond the ken of thought. Being thus self-containing, Suchness knows nothing wanting. It is therefore called the *Tathagata-garbha*, 'womb of Tathagatahood', and the Tathagata's Dharmakaya.

'A question may be asked: when Suchness is regarded as always retaining, when in itself, the nature of the sameness, free from all differentiating features, how is it possible to describe it as in possession of such a variety of virtues?

'The answer is: While it truly contains all these virtues, there is no differentiation in them, they are all of sameness, of one taste, of one Suchness. Why? Because of non-discrimination (which characterises Suchness), there is neither that which discriminates nor that which is discriminated. Therefore, Suchness is non-dualistic.

'If non-dualistic, where does differentiation come in? It is due to our Karma-consciousness whereby things are presented to us in the aspect of birth and death.

'How does this presentation take place? All things are primarily of the Mind only, in which there is no awakening of thoughts. But mentation somehow moves in the wrong direction, and there is the rising of thoughts whereby the world is perceived in all its multitudinousness. Thus ignorance is talked about. When the Mind remains in and with itself and has no rising (of thought) it is the great light of Prajna. When there is the rising of perception in the Mind some things are perceived while others remain unperceived; but the Mind in itself stands outside perception and for this reason it universally illumines the world. When the Mind moves, its knowledge ceases to be true as it deviates from itself; it is then neither eternal, nor blissful, nor self-seeking, nor free from defilement; on the contrary it burns, it suffers pain, it becomes subject to decay and change, it is no more free; and then there will be all kinds of errors and defilements. Contrariwise, when the Mind moves not, there will be all kinds of pure virtues manifested. So when the Mind is stirred and perceives things before it as objects of thought, it will find in itself something lacking. Just because no thoughts are stirred in the One Mind it is the repository of virtues innumerable, pure and meritorious, and because it is thus self-contained and wanting nothing it is called the womb of Tathagatahood, that is, the Dharmakaya.'

From these quotations from Asvaghosha, who is representative of the Mahayanists of India and whose doctrine has been one of the greatest factors which have moulded the thought of Chinese and Japanese Buddhists, we can see in what relationship the idea of Suchness stands to the Mind, Prajna, Enlightenment, Void, Womb of Tathagatahood, and Dharmakaya, and further to ignorance, discrimination, the rising of thoughts, the recognition of an objective world, and defilements so-called. The Mahayana does not deny the world objective and subjective, for it is Suchness as it is. It becomes the opportunity of defilements when it is discriminated in the direction of dualism and not in the direction of Suchness. Dualism is asserted as soon as a thought rises and its absolute validity is upheld, which is known as wrong attachment. Enlightenment takes place when dualism is recognised in the light of Suchness. This leads us to the consideration of Nirvana.

3 NIRVANA

Nirvana as Void has been one of the thoughts constantly subjected to misunderstanding by the Western critics of Buddhism. It is to be stated at the outset that Nirvana has been used in two senses and that when they are confused Nirvana loses its meaning in the philosophy of the Mahayana.

What are the two senses of Nirvana? The word originally meant 'extinction,' as when we speak of a fire which has burned all the fuel. As all the conditions that have made the existence of a fire possible have ceased, the fire itself is extinguished. This is a state of Nirvana. Likewise, when all the evil passions rising from egoism and consequently from dualism are subdued or uprooted, the mind regains its original purity and grace and becomes altogether free from worries and other annoyances. This is Nirvana. Here Nirvana stands against Samsara, birth and death, because it is due to the working of Samsara and our attachment to it that we become victims of mental disturbances and defiling influences. Samsara is dualism, as it is the thought of birth and death, and as long as we are attached to this thought and remain unaware of the truth that there are no such things as birth and death, and that we are really all of Suchness, eternally abiding in the self-sameness of the One Mind, we are never free and never at peace with ourselves as well as with the world. So we come quite frequently across such sentences as 'Avoid the pain of birth and death and seek the bliss of Nirvana' or 'Nirvana is realised only when the root of the evil passions is removed'.

When the Mahayana developed, a new interpretation of Nirvana was adopted. Nirvana was no longer something to be sought outside Samsara, that is to say it did not stand against Samsara. When the idea of Suchness opened up a wider outlook for the Mahayanists, Samsara as well as Nirvana found their places in Suchness itself, and Nirvana was Samsara and Samsara Nirvana. Thus we read in the *Awakening of Faith* that 'Because of the Tathagatagarbha there is Samsara and again because of the Tathagatagarbha there is Nirvana'; again, 'The self-nature of the five Aggregates is unborn and therefore knows no death, because they are primarily Nirvana'; and again, 'The Bodhisattva once awakened to the Bodhicitta is altogether free from cowardice. . . . Even when he learns that Nirvana is obtainable only after a continued life of ascetic mortifications through innumerable aeons he is not at all discouraged, for he knows that all things are from the very beginning Nirvana.' All these thoughts are in agreement with the doctrine of Suchness as expounded above.

Nirvana is thus Samsara, and no more a transcendental entity to be sought after death or to be reached after crossing the stream of Samsara, birth and death. We who are supposedly living a life of eternal becoming are Nirvana itself. All that we need do, therefore, is to find ourselves. This idea of Nirvana has revolutionised the whole trend of Mahayana thought. While the old usage has not yet died, we must accommodate ourselves to the new situation if we wish correctly to understand the Mahayana.

The sutras will be quoted to show the various interpretations given to Nirvana until in the Mahayana it came to be identified with the highest truth or reality, the Dharmakaya itself, and then with Suchness and Enlightenment.

In the Agamas (corresponding to the Pali Nikayas) Nirvana is said to be the state of a complete extinction in which there is no more greed, no more anger, no more folly, nor all the other evil desires and passions. This is the usual Hinayana understand-

ing of the word. In the *Mahavibhasha-Sastra* the etymological
analysis of the term is given with its various religious implications.
When the root *va* is taken to mean 'to blow', 'to move', 'to walk',
or 'to emit a scent', Nirvana is the negation of all these qualities,
that is 'no more stirring of passions', 'the disappearance of form',
'being freed from the evil paths' and 'the cessation of the nauseat-
ing odour'. When *vana* means 'a forest', Nirvana is 'getting out
of the forest of the Aggregates'. When *vana* is considered to be
a derivative of the root *ve*, which means 'to weave', Nirvana is
'the no more weaving of the cloth of birth and death'. When an
Arhat reaches the stage of No-learning he is freed from karmic
laws, and no more weaves the conditions leading to Samsara.
When *vana* means 'birth', Nirvana is 'no-rebirth', 'going to the
other side of the stream'. When *vana* is derived from the root *vr*,
meaning, 'to cover' or 'to obstruct', Nirvana is 'non-obstruction',
emancipation', 'freedom'.

In the Mahayana sutras, on the other hand, Nirvana acquires
a positive significance; it is no more a negative state but something
existing by itself; it is Reality, from which all Buddhas issue.
In the *Mahayana Nirvana Sutra* (Fas. VI) we read: 'It is not
quite right, it is inadequate to state that the Tathagata's entrance
into Nirvana is like a fire going out when the fuel is exhausted.
It is quite right to state that the Tathagata enters in the Dharma-
nature itself.' Again, we have in Fas. IV of the same canon:
'When there is no more oil, the light goes out, but it means only
the going out of the evil passions; as to the oil-container itself,
it remains there. Likewise the Tathagata has all his evil passions
extinguished but his Dharmakaya remains for ever.' The Lotus
Gospel echoes the same idea when it states that the Tathagata's
entrance into Nirvana is one of his 'skilful means', for he stays
here with us for ever to preach his gospel. In other Mahayana
sutras Nirvana is identified with the Dharmakaya, or with the
Dharmadhatu where all Buddhas have their being, or with the
Buddha's deepest meditation, or with Prajnaparamita.

The *Suvarnaprabjasa* (Chinese translation) gives many reasons
why we have to speak of Nirvana, and the following are some of
them: (1) All evil passions rise from greed, but Tathagatas are
free from greed, and this is called Nirvana; (2) As they are free
from greed, they are not attached to anything, and as they are

not attached they neither come into being nor go out of being, and this is called Nirvana; (3) As they neither come into being nor go out of being, they are of the Dharmakaya which abides for ever, and this is called Nirvana; (4) What is thus above birth and death is beyond description, and this is called Nirvana; (5) There is neither subject-ego nor object-world, and all that we see about us is due to the constant changing of conditions, and what is not changeable is called Nirvana; (6) All evil passions are caused by errors and have nothing to do with the Dharma-nature, which is the master neither coming into being nor going out of being. This is known to the Buddha and called Nirvana; (7) Suchness alone is real and all the rest are not. By Suchness is meant Reality, which is the Tathagata and called Nirvana; (8) In Reality there is nothing of falsehood subject to argumentation, and this is understood by the Tathagata alone and called Nirvana; (9) What is unborn is real, what is born is unreal, and the ignorant are drowned in the ocean of birth and death, while the Tathagata is above it, which is called Nirvana; and (10) What is unreal rises from conditionality, whereas Reality transcends it, and the Tathagata's Dharmakaya is this Reality, which is called Nirvana.

What distinguishes the Hinayana conception of Nirvana from that of the Mahayana is the fact that the latter recognises the existence of a reality which stands by itself, pure and undefiled, perceived only by the transcendental intelligence of the Buddha. The Hinayana has no such metaphysically conceived Nirvana, as it is interested only in the extirpation of the evil passions rising from the individual ego-entity, and has not made further inquiries into the philosophical possibility of such experiences.

It has stopped short at the negation, whereas the Mahayana wanted to grasp something positive, whereby alone the Buddhist life becomes possible.

4 TRIKAYA: THE THREE BODIES OF THE BUDDHA

The heart of the Mahayana lies in the Trikaya (Three Bodies of the Buddha) and the Bodhisattva, along with the conception of Prajna (wisdom) and Karuna (compassion).

Soon after the Buddha passed away many of his followers began to think of him as more than a human being. To the Hinayanists the Buddha was a superior human being who attained the perfection of wisdom in this life through the power of his spiritual culture and the accumulated merit of his past lives. 'But the deep reverence which was felt by his disciples could not be satisfied with this prosaic humanness of their master and made him something more than a mortal soul. So even the Pali tradition gives him a supramundane life besides the earthly one.'*

The Mahasanghikas conceived of the Buddha as supramundane and transcendent, and their conception passed over to the Mahayanists who thought of the Buddha in three ways, namely

1   Nirmanakaya (*Nirmana,* transformation; *kaya,* body). As the human Sakyamuni who walked this earth and preached to his fellows and passed away at eighty years of age.
2   Sambhogakaya (*Sambho,* enjoyment; *bhoga,* to partake; *kaya,* body). As the Buddha ideal who enjoyed a refulgent body and preached to the Bodhisattvas.
3   Dharmakaya (*Dharma,* law, substance; *kaya,* body). As the highest being, comprising all others, the essence of knowledge and compassion, the Absolute.

The Buddha is not three but One. The Trikaya are but aspects of the One Buddha. When viewed from the Absolute and Universal point of view, he is the transcendent Dharmakaya; when viewed from the point of view of Ideality, as the human made divine, as it were, he is the Sambhogakaya, preacher to the Bodhisattvas to help them in their work of saving sentient beings; when viewed from the human point of view he is the Nirmanakaya, the historical Sakyamuni who was born in Kapilavastu, obtained enlightenment under the Bodhi-tree, and passed away into Nirvana when his life's work was done.

It must be remembered that Sakyamuni was not the only manifestation of the Dharmakaya in the form of the Nirmanakaya Buddha, for there have been many manifestations of the Nirmanakaya, just as there are many ideals of the Sambhogakaya

* Suzuki, *Outlines of Mahayana Buddhism,* p. 270.

but only one Dharmakaya, the Absolute Buddha, of which the others are only aspects.

In the *Kayatraya*, Ananda relates the Buddha's discourse on the Trikaya. 'Has the Blessed One a body?' Buddha answered, 'The Tathagata has three bodies.' So we can see that the three bodies are three aspects of the one Buddha or Tathagata. They are one in essence, but distinct in their nature and activity.

NIRMANAKAYA

The Nirmanakaya is the Universal Buddha manifested in the world of sentient beings, adapting himself to earthly conditions, possessing an earthly body yet maintaining purity. He is the representative of the Absolute in the human world, bent on teaching sentient beings in order to relieve them from suffering, and through enlightenment to lead them to salvation. In this wise the Buddha teaches and delivers all sentient beings through his religious teachings, whose number is innumerable as the atoms. His all-swaying compassion, intelligence and will cannot rest until all beings have been brought under his shelter through all possible means of salvation. Whatever his subjects for salvation and whatever his surroundings, he will accommodate himself to all possible conditions and achieve his work of enlightenment and salvation.

The Nirmanakaya is generally rendered as Transformation Body, because this body as used in manifestation by Sakyamuni and other human Buddhas partakes of the characteristics and qualities of mortality, and is subject like that of other mortals to sickness, old age and death. The human Buddha expresses the perfect man, pure, wise and wielding power. He is possessed of all the marks of physical excellence, having strength combined with beauty, and his mind is a union of intelligence and compassion.

Gradually the conception of the Nirmanakaya grew larger and more ideal. The historical Buddha who lived among men but who seemed superhuman to his devoted followers in time assumed more and more the form of the ideal Buddha. As in Christianity we find the glorified Christ, so in Buddhism we find the idealised Buddha.

In Hinayana Buddhism the historical Buddha is revered as a

man among men, yet we discern the tendency to idealise him. In Mahayana there is frankly a preference for the ideal Buddha, the Sambhogakaya who preaches to the Bodhisattvas as the Nirmanakaya preaches to ignorant mankind. But although the Nirmanakaya Buddha bears a human body he is of the same nature as the Dharmakaya, indeed a manifestation of him, and in this respect divine or, as the Buddhist would prefer to say, of true Buddha nature. The real body of the Nirmanakaya is the Dharmakaya, and all Nirmanakayas are united in the Dharmakaya.

The Awakening of Faith says: 'The Nirmanakaya depends on the phenomena-particularising consciousness, by means of which the activity is conceived by the minds of common people, Sravakas and Pratyeka-buddhas. This aspect (of the Dharmakaya) is called the Body of Transformation (Nirmanakaya).'

Nirmanakaya Buddhas are to be found everywhere and at all times. The Nirmanakaya body is the vehicle for the activity of the Tathagata, and wherever and whenever he sees best to manifest himself as a Nirmanakaya Buddha he does so. This brings us to the conception of the two forms of the Nirmanakaya, the Ojin and the Keshin, full manifestations and partial ones. The Ojin is practically the active Tathagata, but the Keshin is an ordinary man who reveals an extraordinary amount of the indwelling Buddha spirit. For example, such men as Shotoku Taishi, the founder of Buddhism in Japan, Kobo Daishi, the Shingon saint,* Honen Shonin and Shinran Shonin, founders of the Jodo and Shin sects respectively, would be considered as Keshin, while Sakyamuni would be regarded as Ojin.

The Keshin can manifest itself as a Bodhisattva, as a *deva,* an angel or a superior human being. When we find living in this world, at any time, pure-hearted persons who are working solely for the good of sentient beings (not only for human beings but for animal beings as well) there we find Keshin Nirmanakaya Buddhas. They are those who are trying to alleviate suffering or giving out high teaching, active workers as well as those who are striving to help by giving the example of exemplary lives, not for the sake of self-merit but with the whole-hearted desire to

---

* Except by his own followers, i.e., believers in Shingon, who consider Kobo Daishi to be more than Keshin, no other than a manifestation on earth of Maitreya, the next Buddha to be.

save others. All these are Nirmanakayas of the Keshin type. They are often found in humble positions and their work is sometimes unknown and unappreciated by their fellowmen, they themselves perhaps being unaware of their high rank and their superior attainment. To be such a Bodhisattva should be the desire of every devoted Mahayanist.

SAMBHOGAKAYA

The Nirmanakaya is a manifestation for the benefit of more or less ignorant beings, such as Sravakas, Pratyekabuddhas and Bodhisattvas of lower ranks, but the Sambhogakaya is manifested for the benefit of all Bodhisattvas. It is the Sambhogakaya who is the preacher of most of the Mahayana sutras, except the Shingon, which claims to be teaching given directly by the Dharmakaya Buddha.

The Sambhogakaya is sometimes called the Body of Recompense because it enjoys the fruits of its spiritual labours, but later it was called the Body of Bliss because it is enjoyed by all the Bodhisattvas. The Sambhogakaya is visible to the Bodhisattva. It is a symbol of transcendental perfection and personifies Wisdom. It is the Buddha ideal.

This Buddha Body is a refulgent body from which are emitted rays of light. It has two forms, the first for its self-enjoyment, the second for the teaching of the Bodhisattva. 'This last body is in possession of wonderful spiritual powers, reveals the Wheel of Dharma, resolves all religious doubts raised by the Bodhisattvas and lets them enjoy the bliss of the Mahayana Dharma.'*

The Sambhogakaya is an expression of the Dharmakaya and stands between the Dharmakaya and the Nirmanakaya. To many minds, the Dharmakaya is unthinkable, but the Sambhogakaya is thinkable. So to some, the Sambhogakaya takes the form of Amida in his Pure Land, to others he is the Christian God, to others again. Isvara. He is, on the one hand, the Buddha idealised, on the other, the Dharmakaya personified. There are some who would compare the Sambhogakaya to the glorified Christ, but rather is it like the Christian God, in distinction to the Absolute

* Suzuki's *Outlines*, p. 266.

Godhead. Amida in his Pure Land and God in his Heaven – both are the Sambhogakaya.

The Sambhogakaya is the Eternal Buddha, and many Mahayanists turn to him rather than to the historical Sakyamuni, who is his mouthpiece or shadow. They have been blamed for this, but they retort that they prefer the substance to the shadow, the reality to the image. The Sambhogakaya, they point out, was incarnated in the Nirmanakaya, and when our eyes are open to the glory of the Eternal Buddha we need not look at his human expression. In the days of our ignorance the teaching and example of the human Buddha are helpful to us, but when we see clearly with the eyes of a Bodhisattva, and 'not through a glass darkly' we look to the refulgent Buddha, the Buddha of Light, of Truth, of Eternality.*

DHARMAKAYA

The general explanation is that the Dharmakaya (*Hosshin*) is the permanent, undifferentiated, comprehending Truth, but the detailed explanation differs according to the different schools of Buddhism. In *The Awakening of Faith*, we read that it is Primary Truth. The Prajnaparamitas take the Dharmakaya as produced by the *dharma*, the highest being; the Dharmakaya is Prajna, the highest knowledge. Eon in the *Daijogisho* says of the Dharmakaya that it is the beginningless body of Being itself. In the *Butsujikyo*, we read that Dharmakaya is the Tathagata's self-nature body, permanent and unchanging, the real nature of every Buddha and every being. The Madhyamika meant by the Dharmakaya the Void, which may, however, mean Reality which cannot be expressed in words. The Yogacaras meant the Absolute.

Shingon regards the Dharmakaya as personal, manifesting compassion and activity, and saving beings by preaching to them, not only as impersonal and transcendental. It is not formless but is real substance, true and permanent. The Dharmakaya is the sum-total of the substance of the Universe. The Dharmakaya manifests itself in the universe in and through all its parts,

---

* 'The Sambhogakaya manifesting itself everywhere is infinite, boundless, limitless, unintermittent in action and embraces infinite attributes of bliss and merit.' *Awakening of Faith*, pp. 101–102.

and this manifestation works actively in law and in form. The Dharmakaya is the inner enlightened body of Buddha. To the ignorant it is formless, but to those who understand it the Dharmakaya has form and preaches the Law. According to general Buddhism the Dharmakaya is absolutely formless and tranquil, but Shingon stresses the supreme enlightenment which expresses itself actively in compassion and thus forms a true personality which the enlightened person can perceive and know.

Reality is probably the best way to describe the Dharmakaya in one word. It is that which must be realised by every being for himself. It is the goal of Bodhisattvas and others, although as a rule only a Bodhisattva can hope to realise it fully. Every being possesses it. It is the real nature of things, and from this aspect of it we can also call it Tathata, Dharmadhatu, Tathagatargarbha. Nirvana is its abode. 'Dharmakaya is literally a body or person that exists as principle, and it has now come to mean the highest reality from which all things derive their being and lawfulness, but which in itself transcends all limiting conditions. It is what inwardly and essentially constitutes Buddhahood.'*

In the *Lankavatara* the Dharmakaya signifies the Buddha-personality when it is perfectly identified with the Dharma or the absolute truth itself.

In *The Awakening of Faith* the Dharmakaya is 'the eternal, the blessed, the self-regulating, the pure, the tranquil, the immutable and the free. Suchness is called the Tathagata's Womb (*tathagatagarbha*) or the Dharmakaya. The activity of the Dharmakaya has two aspects, the first depending on the phenomena-particularising consciousness by means of which the activity is conceived by the minds of common people, Sravakas and Pratyekabuddhas. The second depends on the activity-consciousness (*karmavijnana*) by means of which the activity is conceived by the minds of Bodhisattvas while passing from their first aspiration stage (*cittotpada*) up to the height of Bodhisattva-hood. This is called the Body of Bliss (*sambhogakaya*).'

Some writers on Mahayana give to the Dharmakaya the idea of Shinnyo (Suchness), the principle of the cosmos, but writers like D. T. Suzuki make the Dharmakaya much more personal. He insists that to Suchness is added a living spirit with virtues.

* D. T. Suzuki in *Studies in the Lankavatara*, p. 308.

This is also the teaching of Shingon. 'The Dharmakaya is a soul, a willing and knowing being, one that is will and intelligence, thought and action. It is not an abstract metaphysical principle like Suchness, but it is a living spirit that manifests in nature as well as in thought. Buddhists ascribe to the Dharmakaya innumerable merits and virtues and an absolute perfect intelligence, and make it an inexhaustible fountainhead of love and compassion.'*

The *Avatamsaka Sutra* makes a comprehensive statement concerning the nature of the Dharmakaya as follows:

The Dharmakaya, though manifesting itself in the triple world, is free from impurities and desires. It unfolds itself here, there, and everywhere, responding to the call of karma. It is not an individual reality, it is not a false existence, but is universal and pure. It comes from nowhere, it goes to nowhere; it does not assert itself, nor is it subject to annihilation. It is forever serene and eternal. It is the One, devoid of all determinations. This Body of Dharma has no boundary, no quarters, but is embodied in all bodies. Its freedom or spontaneity is incomprehensible, its spiritual presence in things corporeal is incomprehensible. All forms of corporeality are involved therein; it is able to create all things. Assuming any concrete material body as required by the nature and condition of karma, it illuminates all creations. Though it is the treasure of intelligence it is void of particularity. There is no place in the universe where this Body does not prevail. The universe becomes, but this Body forever remains. It is free from all opposites and contraries, yet it is working in all things to lead them to Nirvana.

It benefits us by destroying evils, all good things thus being quickened to growth; it benefits us with its universal illumination which vanquishes the darkness of ignorance harboured in all beings; it benefits us through its great compassionate heart which saves and protects all beings; it benefits us through its great loving heart which delivers all beings from the misery of birth and death; it benefits us by the establishment of a good religion whereby we are strengthened in our moral

* D. T. Suzuki, *Outlines of Mahayana Buddhism*, pp. 222-3.

activities; it benefits us by giving us a firm belief in the truth which cleanses all our spiritual impurities; it benefits us by helping us to understand the doctrine by virtue of which we are not led to disavow the law of causation; it benefits us with a divine vision which enables us to observe the metempsychosis of all beings; it benefits us with an intellectual light which unfolds the mind-flowers of all beings; it benefits us with an aspiration whereby we are enlivened to practise all that constitutes Buddhahood. Why? Because the Sun-Body of the Tathagata universally emits the rays of the Light of Intelligence.*

From all this Suzuki claims that 'the Dharmakaya is the *raison d'être* of all beings, transcends all modes of *Upaya,* is free from desires and struggles and stands outside the pale of our finite understanding'.

Suzuki also puts emphasis upon the intelligent mind and loving heart of the Dharmakaya. Here he approaches the Shingon interpretation.

The Dhamakaya which is tantamount to Suchness or Knowledge of Suchness is absolute; but like the moon whose image is reflected in a drop of water as well as in the boundless expanse of the waves, the Dharmakaya assumes in itself all possible aspects from the grossest material form to the subtlest spiritual existence. When it responds to the needs of the Bodhisattva whose spiritual life is on a much higher plane than that of ordinary mortals, it takes on itself the Body of Bliss or Sambhogakaya. This Body is a supernatural existence, and almost all the Buddhas in the Mahayana scriptures belong to this class of being.

The Mahayanists now argue that the reason why Sakyamuni entered into Parinirvana when his worldly career was thought by him to be over is that by this resignation to the law of birth and death, he wished to exemplify in himself the impermanence of worldly life and the folly of clinging to it as final reality. As for his Dharmakaya, it has an eternal life; it was never born, and it will never perish, and when called by the

* D. T. Suzuki, *Outlines of Mahayana Buddhism,* pp. 223–37.

spiritual needs of the Bodhisattvas, it will cast off the garb of absoluteness and preach, in the form of a Sambhogakaya, 'never-ceasing sermons which run like a stream for ever and aye'. It will be evident from this that Buddhists are ready to consider all religious or moral leaders of mankind, whatever their nationality, as the Body of Transformation of the Dharmakaya.*

We have two conceptions or rather two ways of stressing the one conception: (1) Dharmakaya is Suchness (*Bhutatathata*), the Body of the Law, the Impersonal Absolute; (2) Womb of Tathagata (*Tathagatargarbha*); true knowledge and the source of every individual being, underlying all phenomena, endowed with Love, Compassion and Will, therefore personal.

The Dharmakaya corresponds to the Godhead in Christianity.

The Buddha impressed upon his followers that the true body of the Buddha is not his human but his spiritual body, that is to say the Dharmakaya is his true body. His immediate followers, however, understood this to mean a body of dharmas, but gradually they thought of the Dharmakaya as the essence of all dharmas, hence the essence of existence itself and of Absolute Wisdom. As beings cannot perceive the Dharmakaya except through spiritual experience, it takes the form of the Sambho-gakaya for beings of the Bodhisattva type and of the Nirmanakaya for ordinary beings. The Dharmakaya is the representative of Shinnyo (Suchness), the impersonal and absolute unity of the Universe.

The Dharmakaya is also the spiritual body of all the Tathagatas.

All this may seem complicated, but in reality it is not. In philosophical Christianity God is considered in his unknowable aspect as the Godhead, the source of all, yet not realisable except through mystical experience. This is the Dharmakaya. That beings may come in contact with him he becomes God as usually known to all Christian believers; this corresponds to the Sambhogakaya. But ordinary people need something more tangible and require

---

* D. T. Suzuki, *Outlines of Mahayana Buddhism*, pp. 258–61.

a living personality. This is the Nirmanakaya to Buddhists and Christ to Christians.

If looked at in this way, the mystery of the Three Bodies disappears. In Indian phliosophy we find Dharmakaya as both Parabrahman and Brahman, according to the aspect that is considered. Sambhogakaya is the same as Isvara, and Nirmana-kaya applies to the great spiritual leaders of India, or may be considered as an Avatar. Instead of three bodies, it may make it clearer to speak of three aspects of the one Buddha: the Historical, the Eternal and the Universal, that is to say: (1) Sakyamuni, the historical Buddha, (2) the Eternal Buddha, as personified by Amida or Akshobhya, and whether considered as Isvara, God or any other Eternal Form, and (3) the Dharmakaya as taught in Shingon, unknowable except through spiritual experience and difficult for any but the Bodhisattva to perceive. By meditation or worship on any one of these aspects – and what is worship but a form of meditation? – beings may come to realise the Existence of the Infinite for themselves.

To explain the Trikaya in words is difficult, and meditation on the problem will reveal far more than the printed page. But to understand Mahayana Buddhism some understanding of the Triple Body conception is necessary. It underlies all Mahayana teachings and is preached or taken for granted in Mahayana sutras. Whether we read the *Pundarika* or the *Prajna*, the *Lanka* or the *Avatamsaka*, this doctrine pervades all the teachings of the great sutras.

5 AMIDA

Amida (Amitabha), the Buddha of Eternal Light and Infinite Life, is the form of the Buddha worshipped in the Pure Land schools of Buddhism, such as Jodo and Shin.

When the heart of Sakyamuni, filled with love for all mankind, was about to preach the doctrine of great bliss for the salva-tion of all beings, his face shone beautifully, and his whole figure became as serene as an autumn cloud, and inspired Ananda to ask Buddha the question as above cited. The word came from Ananda's own lips, but the spirit of the Master was plainly visible in them. The heart of Sakyamuni, which reached the highest pinnacle of purification, naturally moved Ananda, who was his beloved disciple, and made his heart reflect like a looking-glass what was going on in the Buddha's heart. Ananda understood the supreme state of 'mutual contemplation of the Tathagatas'. To get a good crop of grain, there must first be a well tilled field prepared for sowing seeds. So the appearance of a great spiritual movement in the world is to be preceded by well cultivated minds that are ready to receive the doctrine of a Holy One; for then the latter will find it easy to penetrate thoroughly into their hearts. The time was ripe now, besides the monastic religion of self-enlightenment and penance, for the seed of a religion of salvation by faith to grow and bear fruit in the well cultivated minds of the Mahayana Buddhists.

Thus was opened the way to the doctrine of salvation by faith.

The Saviour of the Shin-shu as the object of faith may be said to resemble to a certain extent the God of Christianity. But Amida's attitude towards sin is what distinguishes the Shin-shu from Christianity. The God of the latter is a God of love and justice, while the Buddha is mercy itself and nothing more. In the world the principle of karma prevails, and the Buddha never judges. The God of Judaism was represented by Christ to be the God of love, yet he is made to judge our sins and mete out punishments accordingly. Amida of the Shin-shu, however, knows only of infinite love for all beings, wishing to deliver them out of the eternal cycle of ignorance and suffering, in which they are found migrating. In Amida, therefore, there is no wrath, no hatred, no jealousy.

There is another aspect in the conception of Amida, besides the one we have already referred to; for he is to be interpreted also in the light of the fundamental principle of Buddhism. Amida, as the Tathagata, naturally appears as a person embodying in himself the Absolute Truth, which is also infinite mercy and infinite wisdom.

So Amida, our Saviour, is an absolute being transcending time and space, and manifesting himself in the Pure Land, the only purpose of which is to save all sinful beings. In short, out of the absolute Buddha or the Dharmakaya has the Buddha of salvation appeared, and naturally the spirit of Amida is in deep and intimate communion with the Absolute itself. And on our side, as we are also sharers in the being of the Absolute Buddha, we and Amida must be said to be one in substance, only differing in functions.

Thus we see that there are two aspects in the idea of Amida. First, Amida is the embodiment of the infinite mercy and wisdom which was obtained, according to the moral law of causation, by perfecting himself through discipline, by performing all that is required of man as a moral being, by accumulating all the merits needed for the salvation of all beings, so that when we believe in him we acquire all those virtues which will immediately be transferred to us and will perfect us. Secondly, Amida is conceived as a person embodying the absolute truth in its highest form, which we also realise in various degrees.

Practically considered, Amida as our Saviour is infinite in love, wisdom, and power; he is the culmination of our religious yearnings. Those who believe in him are thus saved from ignorance and suffering, gain enlightenment, and find in him a guide of their daily life.*

The general belief in regard to Amida is that he was once a monk who out of compassion for his fellow beings made vows that he would devote all his own merits, which he had gained by many lives of mercy, to the saving of others. He established a Pure Land where he could receive those souls who believed in him and called upon his name. Amida is the Sambhogakaya – the Body of Bliss who is spoken of as the accommodated Law-Body for the object of Faith. Yet Amida and the Dharmakaya are really one being, two aspects of the one Buddha—the one, Dharmakaya, from the philosophical side; the other, Sambhogakaya, from the religious. Sakyamuni was the representative of the Dharmakaya for the purpose of preaching the Law, and Amida saves sentient beings by means of their faith in him. In the Pure Land sects human life is looked upon as illusory, transitory and miserable

* Quoted from Shugaku Yamabe's article on Amida as Saviour of the Soul, *Eastern Buddhist*, Vol. I, No. 2.

through the action of karma, the law of cause and effect. The only way to be released is to call upon Amida in perfect faith and he will save us by calling us to his Pure Land, which is a field for enlightenment. Amida may therefore be conceived of in three ways: as the Dharmakaya, absolute and unconditioned, as the Sambhogakaya, the idealised, glorified being who is the object of worship in the Pure Land sects, and as the Nirmanakaya, the historical Buddha Sakyamuni who came to preach the Law.

6 BODHISATTVA

The first conception in Mahayana is that of the Bodhisattva. A Bodhisattva is a future Buddha, and we are all future Bodhisattvas, while those who have already taken the Bodhisattva vows are already on the first rung of the ladder of Bodhisattvaship. This thought gives a great impetus to leading the Buddhist life.

There are two views of the Bodhisattva, first in its broader and more popular sense, as the name for those who take the vow to realise their ideals on the way to Buddhahood, and, secondly, as the name for those who are ever striving for the enlightenment of other sentient beings through the practice of the four great vows* and the Paramitas.

Sakyamuni was himself a Bodhisattva, and in the Jataka Tales we are given the stories which tell of his previous lives as animal and as man, in each of which he practised compassion and worked for the welfare of others.

In Hinayana the followers of the Buddha were taught to become not Bodhisattvas but Arhats, but the Mahayanists wanted to make every being like Sakyamuni; they wanted lavishly to distribute the bliss of enlightenment; they wanted to remove all the barriers that were supposed to lie between Buddhahood and common humanity.

The great difference between the Arhat and the Bodhisattva is that the former is intent upon his own enlightenment and liberation, while the Bodhisattva wishes to help all creatures and bring

---

* These four vows are:
1 To save all beings.
2 To destroy all evil passions.
3 To learn the Truth and teach it to others.
4 To lead all beings towards Buddhahood.

them to full enlightenment. In order to do this, although qualified for Nirvana he voluntarily renounces it in order to remain in the world to help all creatures, men and animals.

The first step on the march of the Bodhisattva is the moment when he takes the vows which, according to Santideva in his *Bodhicharyavatara*, are as follows:

1   The sin accumulated in my former existences, accumulated in all creatures, is infinite and omnipotent. By what power can it be conquered if not by the desire of Bodhi, by the desire to become Buddha for the salvation of men? This totally disinterested desire is infinitely sacred. It covers a multitude of sins. It assures happiness during the round of existences. It is a pledge of the supreme happiness of the Buddhas for oneself and one's neighbour. All honour to the Buddhas whom everybody naturally loves and who have as their sole aim the salvation of men!

2   I worship the Buddhas and the Bodhisattvas with a view to undertaking the vow of Bodhi (*vandana*). Possessing nothing, by reason of my sins, how can I render unto them the worship (*puja*) which is their due? But I am wrong. I do possess something. I give myself unreservedly by pure affection to the Buddhas and to their sons, the divine Bodhisattvas. I am their slave and, as such, have no more danger to fear. Of all dangers the greatest is that which comes from my sins. I know how harmful these are; I deplore them; I acknowledge them. I see and you see them as they are; pardon them!

3   But enough of myself. Let me belong entirely to the Buddhas and to creatures. I rejoice in the good actions, which among ordinary men for a time prevent evil rebirths. I rejoice in the deliverance gained by the Arhats. I delight in the state of Buddha and Bodhisattva, possessed by the Protector of the world (*punyanumodana*). I entreat the Buddhas to preach the Law for the salvation of the world (*adhyesana*). I entreat them to delay their entrance into Nirvana (*yacana*). All the merits acquired by my worship of the Buddhas, my taking of refuge, my confession of sins I apply to the good of creatures and to the attainment of Bodhi.

I wish to be bread for those who are hungry, drink for those who are thirsty (*parinamana*). I give myself, all that I am and shall be in my future existences, to all creatures (*atmabhava-parityaga*). In the same dispositions as those in which the former Buddhas were when they undertook the vow of Bodhi, and just as they carried out the obligations of future Buddhas, practising in their order the perfect virtues in these dispositions, I conceive the desire for Bodhi for the salvation of the world. So also I shall practise in their order my obligations (*cittot-pada*), or vows (*pranidhi*).

Further than this first period few can go in this world of relativity, but it may be interesting to consider the ten stages of the Bodhisattva.

The first is that of joy (*Pramudita*). He feels joy because by the fruit of his actions and meditation he is born in the family of Buddha; he feels joy in his affection for the Buddhas and joy in the fact that he is devoting himself to the work of a Bodhisattva; he also takes joy in his feeling of good will to all creatures and to the vow which he has made. Fears disappear, and he devotes himself to honouring the Buddhas, helping all creatures and preaching the Law. His chief thought is not: 'May I become a Buddha and attain Nirvana'; but 'May I become a Buddha in order to help every creature who may have recourse to me.' Here we are reminded of Amida and his vows, especially his eighteenth, namely, 'O Bhagavat, if those beings who have directed their thought towards the highest perfect knowledge in other worlds and who, having heard my name, when I have obtained Bodhi (knowledge), have meditated on me with serene thoughts; if at the moment of their death, having approached them, surrounded by an assembly of Bhikshus, I should not stand before them, wor-shipped by them, that is, so that their thoughts should not be troubled, then may I not attain the highest, perfect knowledge.'

In our own lives we can cultivate this aspect of joy; we can make an imitation of the Bodhisattva even though we cannot practise it as yet perfectly. The religious life should be joyful; the very thought of belonging to the family of Buddha ought to bring the greatest happiness, and, as many sutras say, perfume our lives with all their thoughts and actions. To take this seriously will mean that, as members of the family of Buddha, we must conquer sin and fear and work for the good of others. Then, when others see our joy, they will wish to know the cause of it, and knowledge of its cause will spur them on to secure this joy for themselves.

The second stage of the Bodhisattva is that of the Immaculate (*Vimala*), obtained by the practice of morality. Here again we ordinary beings may strive to imitate the Bodhisattva, practising morality as best we can, and we can do this as we free ourselves from the limited conception of the ego. The Bodhisattva not only lives according to the precepts but urges others to do so, both by teaching and example. Here he is walking in the Eightfold Noble Path.

The third stage is called the Illuminating (*Prabjakari*). Here he reflects upon the nature of things and practises patience, which really means forbearance toward people and things as they are. Patience or forbearance is one of the chief Buddhist (Mahayanist) virtues. To be tolerant and patient with the sins, frailties, vanities and oddities of others is an important virtue. Most of us can imitate the Buddha here with great advantage to ourselves and others.

The fourth stage is called the Radiant (*Archismati*). It is the stage in which the greatest energy must be practised. Here the Buddha practises most strenuously good works as well as meditation, but in the fifth stage (*Sudurjaya*) meditation predominates. Without meditation how is it possible to attain knowledge? Here the Bodhisattva gives us the example of the efficiency and desirability of meditation. Through meditation we can grasp the Truth which leads to the reign of Prajna (Transcendental Knowledge) and to the sixth stage, called the Turned Towards (*Abhimukti*). He is now an Arhat as well as a Bodhisattva. His mind is open and clear and he shines as it were by the light of Prajna.

The Bodhisattva is now a very high being indeed, so high that our ordinary, relative minds cannot follow him. To understand him now we must ourselves stand where he is. The Hinayana does not mention any further stages, but the Mahayana conceives of three more.

The seventh is the Far Going (*Durangama*). He is now skilled in all means of leading others to Bodhi. This stage includes all the fruits of the previous six, and gives the full development of the intelligence of the Bodhisattva. Although he no longer has worldly thoughts he can, through his great compassion, assist others in their troubles in this world, and he turns over his merit to assist them.

The conception of magical bodies in Mahayana is interesting. In order to help beings the Buddha may assume any form he wishes; he may become any kind of man or woman, he may assume the form of a deity in which to appear to a devotee; he may take any form, high or low, if thereby he can carry out his benevolence and mercy, not merely to human beings but to animals and plants and the very dust on which he treads. This is a noble teaching of Mahayana Buddhism, that all life is one and that the Dharmakaya is manifested in all forms. This is why we should treat animals with kindness, and care for plants, rather than think that lower forms of life only exist for the benefit of the higher forms and have no significance of their own. In Mahayana Buddhism all are of value, for all are expressions of the Dharmakaya.

The eighth stage is called the Steadfast or Immovable. Its characteristic is the possession of the supreme knowledge of *Anutpattikadharmaksanti*. It is will in action, the state of a divine mind, a state of consciousness of which we can have no conception. By now the Bodhisattva has lost the idea of duality. His subconscious intelligence is constantly acting in all kinds of merciful ways, but his conscious mind is quiet and serene. This stage gives way to the ninth, that of 'The Good' (*Sadhumati*) and the Preacher of the Law.

In the tenth, Cloud of the Law (the *Dharmamegha*), is the arrival at the End. The Bodhisattva realises the last of the Samadhis and the Buddhas consecrate him. He has now all the powers and characteristics of a Buddha. He is the personification of love and sympathy. He has reached the highest principle next to the Buddha.

He is now enshrined in the heart of the Dharmakaya. The goal is reached, but he is still a Bodhisattva in the sense that he is manifested Dharmakaya who helps creatures and prepares them in turn for Bodhisattvaship and Buddhahood. Such is the splendid teaching of Mahayana in regard to the Bodhisattva.

The aspirant to Buddahood has the perfected Bodhisattva as his ideal, and in the lower stages he can imitate him and in the first stage he can take the first step. Every disciple of the Mahayana aspires to become a Buddha, nor is it necessary to become a monk. Wherever he is, if he possess the resolution he may take the vow before his spiritual teacher or he may take it alone, but in order to take it he must be filled with love and compassion for all creatures, and resolve to practise the Six Paramitas (Virtues of Perfection).

The Paramitas are, first, Dana, generosity, charity, giving, materially in the form of alms, and mental and spiritual giving, too. Writing a book, educating a child, delivering a sermon, preparing a meal, washing dishes, living one's own life as well as possible – these are all *dana,* for these, too, are for the good of all. Dana expresses itself not only in liberality and alms-giving, but in being amiable, and sympathetic for others in their joys and sorrows. It also includes a willingness to give all its acquired merits for the salvation of others.

The second Paramita is Sila, morality or good conduct, to destroy as far as possible all evil passions, not for one's own benefit but in order to insure good rebirths for the purpose of saving others. Mahayana regards the concentration on positive virtues as of more importance than abstention from evil. To the Mahayanist morality means active doing rather than passive refraining.

The third Paramita is Kshanti (patience), which, as mentioned before, is a kind of forbearance. The aspirant to Buddhahood never grows angry, impatient or excited over what is done by ignorant persons, for he must ever keep in mind that all trouble is due to causes.

Energy (*virya*) is the fourth Paramita. In order to tread the Path it is necessary to be energetic and strenuous, not to give way to weakness or discouragement, not to become attached to worldly pleasures, and to keep one's resolutions strong.

The fifth Paramita is Dhyana, contemplation or meditation. Buddhism has many systems of meditation, and Mahayana is especially rich in this field. Whatever method is chosen it is for the purpose of acquiring pure knowledge that will help us on our path and prepare us for the realisation of *paratmasamata*, the knowledge of the equality of oneself and one's neighbour and of the substitution of one's neighbour for oneself; in fact, the realisation of non-ego and the oneness of the Dharmakaya.

The sixth Paramita is Knowledge or Wisdom (*prajnaparamita*) which is the supreme virtue, although to attain it all the other Paramitas must be practised equally. Its complete possession is the same as Nirvana. We ordinary beings can only try to get a glimpse of the full splendour of Prajna which the Bodhisattva reflects.

Four paramitas were later added to the original six: Upaya (skilful means or device), Pranidhana (vow or resolution), Bala (strength or power), Jnana (knowledge). Of these the most important is Upaya. The Bodhisattva is told to use every possible device or expedient to bring beings to enlightenment. D. T. Suzuki in his *Outlines* explains it thus: 'Upaya, meaning "expedient", "stratagem", "device", or "craft", has a technical sense in Buddhism. It is used in contrast to intelligence (*prajna*) and is synonymous with love (*karuna*). So, Vimalakirti says in the *sutra* bearing his name (chap. 8, verses 1–4): "Prajna is the mother of the Bodhisattva and Upaya his father; there is no leader of humanity who is not born of them." Intelligence (*prajna*) is the one, the universal, representing the principle of sameness (*samata*), while Upaya is the many, being the principle of manifoldness (*nanatva*). From the standpoint of pure intelligence, the Bodhisattvas do not see any particular suffering existences, for there is nothing that is not of the Dharmakaya; but when they see the universe from the standpoint of love-essence, they recognise everywhere the conditions of misery and sin that arise from clinging to the forms of particularity. To remove these, they devise all possible means that are directed towards the attainment of the final aim of existence. There is only one religion, the religion of truth, but there are many ways, many means, many *upayas*, all issuing from the all-embracing love of the Dharmakaya and equally efficient to lead the masses to supreme enlightenment and universal good. Therefore, ontologically speaking, this universe, the Buddhists would say, is nothing but a grand display of Upayas by the Dharmakaya that desires thereby to lead all sentient beings to the ultimate realisation of Buddhahood. In many cases, thus, it is extremely difficult to render *upaya* by any of its English equivalents and yet to retain its original technical sense.'

Pranidhana Paramita is displayed by the Bodhisattva when he wills to help beings to universal salvation and makes his vows to do so.

Bala Paramita shows the powers of the Bodhisattva which he works to increase, such as his will, thought, wisdom, practice, patience and knowledge.

Jnana Paramita is similar to Prajna, but Jnana refers more to intellectual knowledge and Prajna to intuition.

We see that the stress in the life of a Bodhisattva or even of an aspirant to Buddhahood is laid on the idea of compassion, on the wish to save others. Even the gaining of knowledge is for this object. The true Bodhisattva has no happiness so great as to deliver creatures from pain and trouble and bring them to salvation, and Nirvana itself pales before such happiness.

The Mahayana Bodhisattva follows Samantabhadra in making these vows:

(19) Let him who is disciplining himself in the exquisite Paramitas never be confused in mind as regards enlightenment; from those sins that are hindering let him be thoroughly freed.

(20) Let me practise in the walks of life emancipation from *karma*, evil passions and from the way of *Maya*; like the lotus that is not stained by water, like the sun and the moon that are not attached to the sky.

(21) Extinguishing all pains in the evil paths, establishing all creatures in Happiness, let me practise (the life of Bhadra) for the benefit of all creatures, as far as there are lands and paths in the ten quarters.

(22) Conforming to the lives of all beings, perfecting the life of enlightenment, and holding up the life of Bhadra, let me discipline myself to the very end of time.

This conception of the loving and merciful Bodhisattva is the highest the mind can have, and those who live in its light cannot help having a radiating influence upon all forms of life and thereby attaining supreme happiness.

Some talk of the Kingdom of Happiness. What is this Kingdom but the mind of the Bodhisattva? Others talk of Heaven or Paradise; what are these but the life of the Bodhisattva? There is no happiness but the life he leads in the midst of suffering creation. Happy is that man who has taken the Vow of Bodhisattvaship and set himself to lead the life. In the rich experience which comes even to the beginner who treads this path is the reward for all the trouble and distress. He who would know something of the Bodhisattva's joy, let him take this first step; thereafter his life will become transformed and he will live in the flame of the light which proceeds from the Dharmakaya Buddha.

7 ENLIGHTENMENT AND SALVATION

The object of the Buddhist life has been from the beginning of its history to attain emancipation (*moksha*) from the bondage of ignorance and *karma*. Emancipation means freedom, and freedom is really one of the four characteristics of Nirvana, permanence: bliss, freedom or self-mastery, and purity. Many unthinking critics of Buddhism have made the mistake of supposing that its aim is to enter into Nirvana, that is, complete annihilation. They argue that as long as life lasts *karma* is unavoidable, owing to ignorance; that our intellect is not comprehensive enough to see all the causes of things, and this partial knowledge inevitably leads to wrong deeds, that is, evil *karma*. Therefore, they say, Buddhists propose to annihilate all life-activities by leading a quiet, uneventful life in an exclusive community. By reducing life to its simplest possible terms, they are saved from the temptations of greed, anger, and folly. Emancipation thus consists in doing nothing, and on death the Buddhist attains complete Nirvana, 'without leaving residues'. Let us consider where the critics are wrong.

The Buddhist life is an open war on bondage, slavery, and attachment of all kinds. But emancipation is not a state of mere negation, for this is merely another form of attachment with an equally binding force. Emancipation is enlightenment whereby dualism or relativity is illumined to its fuller significance. This is achieved by means of Prajna; hence the important role to be played by it in the entire scheme of the Buddhist life.

Enlightenment is used as an English equivalent for Bodhi, which comes from *budh*, the root also of Buddha – the enlightened one. *Budh* means primarily 'to know', 'to be aware of', or 'to be awakened to', and 'awakening' instead of 'enlightenment' may be a better term for that Bodhi which the Buddha attained under the Bodhi-tree. The Buddha was awakened to the truth of Suchness, *tathata*, and saw Reality as it is in itself, *yathabhutam*. This awakening emancipated Prince Siddhartha, son of Suddhodana, from the bondage of ignorance and the despotism of *karma*, and he became the Buddha. The term 'ignorance', therefore, means not to be awakened to the ultimate meaning of life, and this not-being-awakened leads to the whirlpool of birth-and-death where *karma* wields its power.

Emancipation is thus effected by an intuitive awakening, without which there will be no Buddhist life. The Threefold Discipline (*siksha*), recommended by Mahayana as well as Hinayana as constituting the Buddhist life, is meant to lead us to awakening or enlightenment, and, as we have seen, the last of the three is Prajna, showing that it is Prajna which is the efficient cause of enlightenment. Morality (*vinaya*), controlling the life of the Brotherhood, is meant to train the mind and body so that conditions will be prepared for the final awakening of Prajna. But according to the Mahayanists morality alone is not enough. The inner mind must be trained and matured for Prajna by Dhyana discipline, for the former lies deeply buried under a heavy load of discursive understanding.

The Threefold Discipline, however, pertains to the individual, and though suitable for the Arhat will not suffice for the Bodhisattva. Individual emancipation is very desirable indeed, but it is too ego-centred, for all religiously-minded people would wish the merit which accrues from such emancipation to be extended towards all beings and shared with them. This was the reason why the Mahayanists were not satisfied with the Sangha institution, but aspired to put into practice the decision of the Buddha to come out of his Samadhi and postpone his entering Nirvana. The Mahayanists read here the moving of the great loving heart of the Buddha. When he came out into the world to preach his doctrine he appears, according to the records of early Buddhism, to have said nothing about the motive which made him take this memorable step, and early Buddhists, paying too much attention to what their Master actually taught, thereby missed the supreme renunciation, which is the core of all his teachings. To miss this was to miss the most essential and most vital meaning of the spiritual movement which goes by the name of Buddhism. In fact, the so-called Mahayanist movement centred on the person of the Buddha more than the teachings which the earlier Buddhists put into the mouth of their Master. This is the principal reason why the Mahayanists talk so much about Mahakaruna, the great compassionate heart of the Buddha, along with his transcendental wisdom, Mahaprajna. The whole system of the Threefold Discipline, Morality, Meditation, and Wisdom, must have as its motive Love or Compassion, *Karuna*, for thus only does individual emancipation find its meaning. If not for the realisation of this compassion towards all beings in the world, of what avail is the Buddhist life, confined in the cloister of the Brotherhood or Sisterhood?

The doctrine of emancipation must also be the gospel of salvation. The Arhat must become the Bodhisattva, even for his own salvation, because if he is endowed with the Buddha-nature he cannot sit serenely, all alone, at the top of the hill of enlightenment and look down on the suffering multitudes. In spite of his enlightenment he must feel something in him which is not emancipated yet. For the emancipation of this little 'something' at the corner of his heart he must become a Bodhisattva. The doctrine of the Bodhisattva's vows and skilful means is the growth from this 'unemancipated' corner in the Arhat's heart, which in fact is the foundation of the Buddhist life and teaching.

The Buddhist doctrine of vow or prayer (*Pranidhana*) is of great importance in the Mahayana system of teaching, and is closely associated with the idea of Bodhisattvahood. The Bodhisattva's vow is not merely a strong wish to have a thing accomplished; it is an expression of the will innate in each of us which manifests itself when we realise that we are what we are because of what others are. Since this will is part of our being, the Bodhisattva's vow is more than his personal wish given utterance, for it moves his deepest life-impulse, Mahakaruna. Herein lies the source of the teaching of the Pure Land, for we read: 'What is

the Buddha-mind? It is no other than the great loving heart.'
The doctrine of the Pure Land reaches its culmination when
emancipation through enlightenment develops into salvation by
faith alone.

It is truly wonderful to see how the Buddhism of individual
emancipation becomes the Buddhism of universal salvation by
faith. In a way it is natural for some critics to think that Pure
Land Mahayana is not Buddhism at all, but the fault lies with the
critics themselves, for they take Hinayana for the genuine teaching of the Buddha, and forget that an essential element of Buddhism is its conception of the Buddha himself. Mahayana, in
whatever form it is taken, never neglects this central fact, and
always views the teaching of the Buddha in its connection with
his personality. With the Mahayanists the Buddha is more than a
historical figure. Truth is truth whoever utters it, but there are
logical truths and living truths and the latter are those which come
from the mouth of a really great person. Such truths are truly
living and inspiring and creative. It may not, therefore, be quite
right to attempt to trace a logical process of development between
the doctrine of emancipation and that of salvation by faith, but
Buddhism as it lives in the Far East today includes without much
difficulty or friction both emancipation through enlightenment
and unconditioned salvation by faith.

Mahayana Buddhism thus holds out to its followers various
ways of progressing on the Way to Enlightenment or Salvation,
by emphasising:

1 The Way of the Moral Life – practising the Eightfold Noble
   Path;
2 The Way of Contemplation or Meditation, as in Zen, which
   aims at obtaining immediate insight into Truth;
3 The Way of Practice, as in Shingon, which combines the disciplinary way with meditation, and adds practices of devotion
   and knowledge;
4 The Way of Belief or Faith in the Grace of a Buddha, such
   as Amitabha or Akshobhya, whereby the devotee wins salvation by faith in the Grace and Love of Another.

Nagarjuna distinguishes between Difficult Work and Easy Work.
The former is meant for strong, self-reliant characters, and the

latter for those who are conscious of their sinful existence which weighs on them too heavily. For the latter the 'Nembutsu' is recommended, which is a constantly repeated invocation to Amida Buddha. This is considered 'Easy Work' compared with the first, which requires moral austerities, clear intellects and the arduous practice of meditation. This kind of religious life is sometimes known as the teaching of the Holy Path, whereas Easy Work is the teaching of the Pure Land, for the devotees of the Nembutsu are assured of being reborn in the Land of Happiness and Purity. The distinction is also made between Self-power (*Jiriki*) and Other-power (*Tariki*). Followers of the Holy Path are self-reliant, those of the Pure Land rely on the Other for their salvation, the Other being Amitabha or Amida.

Of the Japanese Buddhist sects, the Pure Land sects, Jodo, Shinshu, Ji and Yudzunembutsu are Tariki – all others are Jiriki. Jodo and Shin offer salvation through belief and faith in Amida and his saving grace. Nichiren taught that 'the Lotus Gospel' is in every one of us, and when we realise this truth we come into the presence of the Eternal Buddha and are saved. Yudzunembutsu works out the teaching of Kegon by means of the Nembutsu, for it teaches that when anyone recites the Nembutsu in all sincerity of heart, this sincerity passes over to the sincere heart of the Buddha, and at the same time awakens every one of us finally to enlightenment.

Tendai, Shingon, and Zen offer salvation through enlightenment, which is brought about by moral deeds and meditation, in short by earnest efforts on the part of the practiser.

Chapter 3

Further Development of Mahayana

Two main schools of the Mahayana came into prominence, the Madhyamika, founded by Nagarjuna in the second century and represented in Japan by the Sanron sect, and the Yogacarya or Vijnanavada, founded by Asanga and Vasubandhu in the fourth century. The Madhyamika had grown logically from early Buddhism with its three doctrines of the Middle Path, no permanent ego and the momentary and perishing elements (*dharmas*), but the Madhyamika developed the teaching to the point where not only the individual but also the *dharmas* were declared unreal. Nagarjuna described the supreme reality as Sunyata or the Void, his School being called the Madhyamika because it teaches a Middle Doctrine where existence and non-existence have only relative truth, and true wisdom is the knowledge of the real meaning of the Void. Upon the true meaning of Void depends the understanding of this form of Buddhism, but this doctrine is greatly misunderstood. The Void is void only in the sense that it is free from the limitations of relative knowledge; Enlightenment alone will reveal what it really is.

The Yogacarya School, founded by two great Mahayana scholars, agrees in many points with the Madhyamika. All phenomena originate in the mind and nothing exists but the mind. The Vijnanamatra proceeds, as do the Hinayanists, with the analytical division of the five *skandhas* and the *dharmas*. It differs from the Hinayana in that it insists that not only objects are transitory, but that the substances also are impermanent. According to this system of thought, spirit and matter are one, and all external objects are the outcome of the one mind.

The Alayavijnana is a Sanskrit word meaning 'store mind'. The seeds of all phenomena and objects are comprehended and concluded in the Alayavijnana, and when not in action lie latent. It is like a fine perfume, whose scent penetrates into the innermost part and then extends to the outside, that is to say outer deeds, both good and bad.

According to this philosophy the world is produced from our own mind, and the condition needed for the manifestation of seeds is the law of cause and effect. The Alaya is the substance and causation the means; they combine to create the world and show forth all phenomenal objects. The origin of the operation of causation cannot be known, nor can the beginning of the storing of seeds, and their manifestation. All Buddhism, whether Hinayana or Mahayana, has for its basis the law of cause and effect, and so does away with a personal creator. But there is in Mahayana an Absolute Reality, Shinnyo, which is birthless and deathless and permanently existing. It is the substance of all phenomenal objects and the basis of the relative Alaya, which is its active principle. The Middle Path doctrine asserts the oneness of this world with Shinnyo, and urges us to exert ourselves in this world even though it is full of sorrow. Herein lies its religious significance. Bliss, according to this School, does not consist in deliverance from this world, as the Hinayanist would assert, but in working for it while realising our Oneness with it.

The *Kishinron* or *Awakening of Faith in the Mahayana*, as we shall see later, carries on the teachings of the Vijnanavada with its emphasis upon Suchness(*Bhutatathata*), the Trikaya, and salvation by faith.

Buddhism gradually died out as such in India, but before being reabsorbed by Hinduism it left its mark upon it. Mahayana, however, was probably introduced into China very early, although the traditional story is that it arrived in the reign of Emperor Ming (AD 58–75) who, having seen Buddha in a dream, sent to India to inquire about the doctrine. His envoys returned with numerous sutras and holy objects, as well as two monks to translate the sutras. Of those early works the *Sutra of Forty-two Sections* is the only one left, and this is Hinayanist in tone. In later centuries Buddhism developed wonderfully in China, but although to a great extent it was favoured by the Emperors there were periods when it was persecuted, and many temples, books, and works of art were destroyed.

In AD 520 Bodhidharma came to China from India and founded the sect which, when it later reached Japan, was known as Zen. Chi-i (522–97) founded the Tendai (*T'ien-tai*) Sect in an attempt to harmonise all Buddhist teaching, while faith in the Pure Land teaching of Amitabha began to appear as a school of thought soon after. These three sects became the most prominent and influential and later spread to Korea and Japan.

Mahayana Buddhism can best be studied today from the Japanese side, for in Japan it is still a living, vital religion and studied in all its forms. The Hinayana is studied equally, for Mahayana embraces the Hinayana and then proceeds along its own lines, being noted for its broad and tolerant spirit and its desire to utilise the best that lies in all Buddhist teachings.

Mahayana was first introduced into Japan from Korea, when the King of Kudara sent to the Japanese Emperor some Buddhist books and statues. At first the new religion met with antagonism, but gradually prevailed; the Empress Suiko (AD 593–628) became a Buddhist and the Crown Prince, Shotoku Taishi, promoted Buddhism in every possible way, building temples, importing books and monks and encouraging Buddhist study.

A number of sects were introduced into Japan direct from China, among the earliest being the Sanron, which treats of the Madhyamika doctrine, the Jojitsu (*Satya-siddhi-sastra*), the Hosso (*Yogacarya*), the Kusha (*Abhidharmakosa*) representing Hinayana, Kegon (*Avatamsaka*), and the Ritsu (*Vinaya*).

In the ninth century, the Tendai, founded by Dengyo Daishi, and the Shingon, founded by Kobo Daishi (774–835), were followed by the Pure Land Sects of Jodo and Shin, founded respectively by Honen and Shinran Shonin. Zen, which had been introduced already in the seventh century, established itself in three branches, Rinzai, Soto, and Obaku. The last prominent Japanese sect is the Nichiren, founded by Nichiren Shonin. The Kusha, Jojitsu and Sanron no longer exist.

Chapter 4

Mahayana in Practice

1 PRIESTS, MONKS AND NUNS

Priests and monks in Buddhism are not synonymous terms. Monks and nuns are students undergoing discipline. In Japan they are found chiefly in the Tendai, Shingon, and Zen sects, especially in the last, where the life and discipline is strongly stressed as a prelude to priesthood.

Buddhist priests fall into two classes, those who are scholars and those who are engaged in temple work. Many of the priests connected with the larger temples are themselves scholars, and consequently their scholarship is much appreciated. Others, however, seem more interested in the erection of costly edifices and the images inside them. Yet it must not be forgotten that a religion flourishes most when it is objectified among the people, and the fact that these people are still interested in the building of edifices and images shows that the religion is still living. After all, to the ordinary believer a stately temple housing a beautiful statue of the Buddha is of more meaning than a volume of sermons or translations from the Sanskrit or Pali. Never before, however, have scholars been so busy in writing books and articles and delivering lectures and sermons. Some of these scholars uphold the conventional teaching of the temples, while others deny it and branch into new fields of thought. One tendency is to turn back to Primitive Buddhism under the inspiration of European scholars, but the majority, headed by the Buddhist colleges, remain faithful to Japanese medieval Buddhism. To be true to the spirit of Shinran or of Kobo Daishi, as the case may be, is still their ideal.

With the exception of the Shin sect, which from the beginning advocated marriage, priests were not supposed to marry and carry on a family life. But with the Meiji Restoration (1868–71) this was changed. Government support and protection was largely withdrawn from the temples, and the priests were treated in many ways as laymen and allowed to marry. Except in Zen, most of the priests who are masters of temples are married; invariably so in Shin. In Tendai, Shingon, and Zen those who became abbots of temples or, as in Zen, Zen masters, do not marry, whereas ordinary temple masters, those who preside over a temple and conduct its ceremonies, do. They combine the offices of clergyman and pastor, conduct whatever social service is maintained by the temple, preach its sermons, recite sutras, entertain pilgrims and generally manage its affairs. A son of such a priest generally becomes a priest in his turn. The young monk attends school like any ordinary schoolboy and later enters a Buddhist college. If he belongs to Tendai, Shingon, or Zen, he has certain Buddhist initiation ceremonies to perform, and all priests learn to recite sutras and conduct funeral ceremonies. The Zen monk has a very special training. He first serves as acolyte in some temple and later enters a Zendo, where he remains at least three years leading a life of discipline consisting of meditation and manual work. Later he leaves the Zendo and becomes a priest.

There are nuns as well as monks in all sects except Shin, which, as stated before, advocates marriage for all, but the majority are found in Jodo. Like the monks they usually become nuns quite young. They do not live in large convents, but a few together in a temple, their duties being similar to a monk's in the recitation of sutras, especially for the dead. In addition they engage in various good works.

2　LAYMEN

As often mentioned before, Mahayana Buddhism is primarily a religion for laymen. Priests are really for the purpose of leading and serving laymen, which is according to the Bodhisattva ideal. To become a monk or nun with the idea of leading a solitary life, bent only upon attaining one's own salvation, is considered as the ideal of the Arhat and is not prized by the Mahayanist.

How can a lay Mahayanist practise his religion in Japan? If he belongs to the so-called Jiriki sects he can do so in many ways. In every Buddhist household there is a shrine, where will be found a statue of the Buddha or one of his manifestations, and also the memorial tablets of deceased members of the family. Every day offerings of flowers, incense, tea, and cakes are made, and, in a pious household, a short sutra is recited morning and evening.

Besides these observances before the household shrine, a Mahayana Buddhist will frequently visit temples, especially the one with which he is affiliated. There will be special anniversaries and other ceremonies which he will like to attend, and he may make a pilgrimage to one or more temples away from home. The Tendai believer will wish to visit Enryakuji on Mount Hiei near Kyoto; the Shingon follower will go to Koyasan or visit the eighty-eight shrines of Kobo Daishi in Shikoku; the Shin devotee will wish to kneel in one of the Hongwanji temple halls in Kyoto where Amida is worshipped and Shinran Shonin revered. The Zenshuist will want to visit one of the Zen temples associated with the memory of some great master of the past.

3 MEDITATION

In regard to individual religious practices I have already mentioned sutra reading, sutra copying, recitation of hymns and of the Nembutsu, ceremonies and pilgrimages. There remains the important practice of meditation. In the so-called Tariki sects there is no meditation. The Nichiren does not lay stress upon it, for his teaching is more like that of the Pure Land sects when he says, 'Devote yourself whole-heartedly to the "Adoration to the Lotus of the Perfect Truth", and utter it yourself as well as admonish others to do the same.' So we shall consider meditation as practised by Tendai, Shingon, and Zen. Tendai has a number of subjects for meditation. They are for the most part intellectual, connected with the doctrine, such as meditation on the Triple Truth of Emptiness, Transiency, the Middle Path, and Compassion. Shingon meditation has many sides, but for the most part they belong to the esoteric teaching, and ought therefore to be learned by pupil from teacher, and not from the printed page. The essence of them, however, may be found in the *Nyugaganyu-Kwan*: 'Buddha enters me and I enter Buddha' or 'I am one with Buddha.'

There is also the *Gwachirin-kwan*, the Meditation on the

Moon. A picture of a full moon is placed about four feet away from the practiser, who, seated before it, regards the moon picture as if it were a crystal ball or a mirror, and reflects that the mind is like a moon, which has the aspiration for Buddhahood. In imagination he makes the moon larger and larger until it includes all the world; the mind is in union with the universe. When this realisation has taken place, he proceeds to make the moon slowly smaller and smaller, until it has become the original size; the whole world is then enclosed in his mind. The *Ajikwan* meditation is done with a picture of the Sanskrit character A before the practiser, and is similar to but more complicated than the Moon-meditation.

All Shingon devotees are taught to meditate upon the Five Vows:

1 I vow to save all beings.
2 I vow to bring together wisdom and love.
3 I vow to learn all the Dharmas.
4 I vow to serve all the Buddhas.
5 I vow to attain the highest enlightenment, and to meditate upon these vows.

Shingon meditations are truly Mahayanist, for great stress is laid in the Mahayana upon compassion and the wish to help others.

The Meditation *Shi-muryokwan* is for the purpose of delivering other beings from pain by meditation upon one's own wish or vow to deliver them from suffering, to make them happy, and help them to enlightenment. Shingon also makes use of breathing exercises and *mantras* and *mudras*. The idea of Body (*mudra*), Speech (*mantra*) and Mind (meditation) is an outstanding principle in Shingon doctrine and practice.

In Zen, meditation is highly stressed, but Zen meditation is very different from the concrete forms in Shingon or the intellectual subjects in Tendai. Zen is an endeavour to pull the Truth out of the Unconscious – an intuitive knowledge of Truth,* and

* For the methods of Zen meditation consult the works of Daisetz Teitaro Suzuki: *Essays in Zen Buddhism*, Vols I, II, III, especially I and II, *An Introduction to Zen Buddhism*, *Manual of Zen Buddhism*, and *The training of the Zen Buddhist Monk*.

Zen meditation aims at identifying oneself with the highest reality. It repudiates hypnotic trance, vacuity of the mind and intellectual reasoning. To assist the meditator a *koan* is given. This is a problem, but to the conscious mind it generally consists of a meaningless word or phrase, or else a statement or question which seems nonsense from the ordinary point of view. But the *koan* acts as a kind of hook to which the mind can fasten itself so that it can put aside random thoughts and intellectual reasoning. Examples of *koans* given to beginners are *Mu*, meaning literally 'nothingness', *Sekishu*, 'the sound of one hand', *Soku Shin Soku Butsu*, 'one Mind, one Buddha', *Honrai-nomemmoku*, 'What are your original features before your father and mother gave you birth?', and *Nanimono ka immoni kitaru?*, 'Whence comest thou?'. The *koan* is to be taken by the practiser into his consciousness, and so identified with it that it will eventually reveal its meaning. It is only a means to help him to attain to the goal, to open the spiritual eye.

Most teachers of *Zazen*, as Zen meditation is called, not only teach monks in the Zendo but also laymen, in groups and individually, so that if a lay person wishes to practise Zazen he or she can apply to a qualified teacher, be given a *koan,* and come for interviews to the teacher. Of course the monk has the advantage over the layman in that he leads a quiet, unattached life. Serious laymen, therefore, for the practice of Zazen often retreat for a shorter or longer time to a Zen monastery, and join in the monastic life, or, if that is not possible, try to continue their Zazen practice in a comparatively quiet and undisturbed place.

A certain monk had been given the *koan* of 'Nothingness' (*mu*) by his teacher, who said to him, 'From morning to night you take your courage in your whole body and repeat "nothingness," "nothingnesss". Turn yourself into nothingness, blend yourself with it. If any reason or illusion arise within you, cut them down at once, in consequence of which you will go into meditation and come out into the world which is called enlightenment.'

'So I proceeded,' said the monk, 'and tried to solve the problem in my own way. With reason and delusion I repaired to the monastery a hundred times, only to be denied. Once I explained nothingness as mind, another time as soul, and a third time as emptiness. I tried to solve it from a philosophical or psychological standpoint. Every time I was denied, and now had nothing left to express. But I kept on and did my best. Whether awake or sleeping at work or at rest, I always set the problem before me, until at the very last, when the maple trees in the garden in front of the abbot's room were in full crimson, I reached the final enlightenment.'

In the Tariki sects, Jodo and Shin, and also in Nichiren, meditation is not specially practised; in fact Shin sees no need of it. The Shin follower practises his Buddhism by attending temple ceremonies, making morning and evening observances before the household or individual shrine, listening to sermons, and reading orthodox books. He may recite the *Nembutsu*, if he likes, as an act of thanksgiving.

In Jodo, however, the reciting of the *Nembutsu* is markedly stressed. Honen Shonin taught that it should be recited as often as possible. Where the Shin follower uses his rosary only as a symbol, the Jodo uses it practically to mark *Nembutsu* recitation. He also uses a floor bell which he strikes as he repeats the holy phrase, just as the Nichiren devotee uses a drum when he recites the *Myohorengekyo*.

Chapter 5

Outline of Some Important Mahayana Sutras

It was Nagarjuna who brought out Mahayana from within the Buddhist church to the external world. Some have asserted that he was the compiler of these Mahayana sutras, but he was rather the commentator upon sutras which existed before him, and he systematised them. Mahayana sutras already existed in his time, for he refers to them in his works, such as the *Daichidoron*, his commentary upon the *Prajna Paramita*. Many of these sutras have been lost, but some have been preserved. Among those referred to by Nagarjuna are *Daibonhannya-kyo* (*Prajna Paramita Sutra*), *Myohorenge-kyo* (*Saddharma Pundarika*), *Juji-kyo* (*Dasabhumika*), *Nyuhokkaibon* (*Gandavyuha*), and Amida sutras such as the *Muryoju-kyo, Yuima-kyo* (*Vimalakirti*), and *Shuryogon-sammai-kyo* (*Surangamasamadhi*).

It seems that there were two streams of Mahayana in his time. One developed from the Bodhisattva point of view which was held by lay people, and originated in North India. The sutras of this stream have Buddha and Bodhisattva as the central idea. In South India developed the philosophical aspect with the *Prajna Paramita Sutra* as the centre. Although different in origin, both of these streams of thought have as the central core of their doctrine the vow of the Bodhisattva – to seek enlightenment and to save mankind; in each in the background is the idea of Emptiness (*Sunyata*).

Some of the most important Mahayana sutras will be briefly described.

1 PRAJNA PARAMITA (HANNYA)

This sutra is the most primitive and fundamental of all those dealing with the idea of Emptiness which developed out of the causation theory in Primitive Buddhism. There was a large number of versions of *Prajna Paramita*, such as the *Mahaprajnaparamita*, the *Ashtasahasrika-prajnaparamita*, and the larger and smaller *Prajnaparamita-hridaya*. The earliest translation into Chinese was made about AD 170. Portions of the *Prajnaparamita* are considered to be among the earliest Mahayana works.

Kumarajiva translated different texts of the Prajna Paramita, including the *Ashtasahasrika*, which was the basis of the Prajna Paramita group of literature, but it is the *Vajracchedika (Kongokyo) Prajna Paramita*, also translated by Kumarajiva, which became the most popular, and greatly influenced the Chinese mind. There are several renderings into English, notably by Beal in his *Catena of Buddhist Scriptures*, by Max Muller in his *Sacred Books of the East*, by Gemmell and by D. T. Suzuki. The *Vajracchedika Prajna Paramita* teaches that all objects are illusive, phenomenal, and subjective, the products of our own minds, and ends with the words, 'All composite things are like a dream, a phantasm, a bubble and a shadow, are like a dewdrop and a flash of lightning.' The shortest of the *Prajna Paramita* texts is the *Prajna Paramita Hridaya*, which expresses perfectly the Sunyata conception. It is given here in full, as translated from the Sanskrit by D. T. Suzuki.

When the Bodhisattva Avalokitesvara was engaged in the practice of the deep Prajnaparamita he perceived: there are the five Skandhas; and these he saw in their self-nature to be empty.

O Sariputra, form is here emptiness, emptiness is form; form is no other than emptiness, emptiness is no other than form; what is form that is emptiness, what is emptiness that is form. The same can be said of sensation, thought, confection, and consciousness.

O Sariputra, all things are here characterised with emptiness: they are not born, they are not annihilated; they are not stained, they are not immaculate; they do not increase, they do not decrease. Therefore, O Sariputra, in emptiness there is no form, no sensation, no thought, no confection, no consciousness; no eye, ear, nose, tongue, body, mind; no form, sound, colour, taste, touch, objects; no Dhatu of vision, till we come to no Dhatu of consciousness; there is no knowledge, no ignorance; till we come to where is no old age and death, no extinction of old age and death; there is no suffering, accumulation, annihilation, path; there is no knowledge, no attainment, (and) no realisation; because there is no attainment. In the mind of the Bodhisattva, who dwells depending on the Prajnaparamita, there are no obstacles; and, going beyond the perverted views, he reaches final Nirvana. All the Buddhas of the past, present, and future, depending on the Prajnaparamita, attain to the highest, perfect enlightenment.

Therefore, one ought to know that the Prajnaparamita is the great Mantram, the Mantram of great wisdom, the highest Mantram, the peerless Mantram, which is capable of allaying all pain; it is truth because it is not falsehood: this is the Mantram proclaimed in the Prajnaparamita. It runs: *"Gate, gate, paragate, parasamgate, bodhi, svaha!"* (O Bodhi, gone, gone, gone to the other shore, landed at the other shore, Svaha!).

Although the actual Sutra is a long one its teaching is simple. Its view of Emptiness is not the result of analysis, as in Hinayana, in which individual things are minutely analysed, but a synthetic view, seen by the intuition, which is called Prajna Paramita wisdom. This is different from ordinary wisdom, Vijnana (Japanese *shiki*), for Vijnana is the aggregate of experience based on desire, whereas Prajna transcends Vijnana. This emptiness of life and the world is not to be taken in a nihilistic sense. The sutra does not negate the world as fact, but destroys the world as value based upon individuality. Thus a free and bright world appears before us, and a new light shines upon the former world. A new and fundamental alteration of the value of this life is made. Formerly we suffered; now we transcend suffering. Prajna Paramita, starting from the point of view of the theory of ignorance, makes this theory empty and develops a true world of freedom.

This latter idea is more fully developed in Kegon (*Avatamsaka*), which stressed the teaching of Mind pure by nature.

2 AVATAMSAKA (KEGON)

The standpoint of Kegon is also that of the Mind-Only theory of Prajna Paramita idealism. As Kegon presupposes Prajna Paramita, many of the explanations are the same. The Kegon is important because it is considered to be the teaching given out by the Buddha Sakyamuni three weeks after his Enlightenment when still in a state of meditation and in the Dharmakaya form, and in consequence, his Enlightenment is made the centre of the Sutra's substance.

The scope of this Sutra is magnificent, and on its ocean everything as in a mirror is reflected and revealed. In form it is bold, yet delicate and subtle. It is one of the supreme works of the world.

There are two complete translations, one in sixty volumes by Buddhabhadra of Northern India, made in the Eastern Shin dynasty (AD 418–520) and used by the Kegon sect, and one in eighty volumes by Sikshananda, made in the T'ang dynasty (AD 695–9). The forty-volume translation by Prajna in AD 796–7, called the *Fugengyogwanbon*, 'Practice and Vows of Samantabhadra', corresponds to the *Gandavyuha*. This forty-volume *Kegon* (*Gandavyuha*) together with the *Juji-kyo* (*Dasabhumika*) and other sutras makes a complete *Avatamsaka*.

This sutra is not presented as being preached by Buddha himself, for he is for the most part silent; it is rather a dramatic description of the contents of Enlightenment. The Bodhisattva and deva are active, but their activity is performed under the will of the Buddha, and the infinite varieties of activity shown are a revelation of the Buddha's power. Yet it must be remembered that although he remains silent he is in reality the true actor and preacher, since all the others are performing and speaking through him. Insofar as Buddha is the preacher he is Vairochana, the Supreme Buddha, the Dharmakaya, rather than the historical Buddha Sakyamuni. Exoterically, the Buddha in Enlightenment may mean the mendicant under the Bo-tree, but esoterically he is the pervading and permanent Dharmakaya, and this world is no longer an ordinary world but the universe, Dharmadhatu, consisting of numerous interpenetrating worlds. According to this Sutra the human mind is the universe itself and identical with

Buddha, and it lays down the famous proposition that Buddha, Mind, and Beings are one and the same.

The fifteenth chapter is the Jujihon on the Ten Stages, and describes the stages of the Bodhisattva from 'the cherishing the first thought for enlightenment' to the attainment of full Buddhahood. This chapter forms an independent sutra known as the *Dasabhumika*, and will be treated later.

In the sixteenth chapter the pure deeds of the Bodhisattva are described, and succeeding chapters enlarge upon this theme. The twenty-fifth chapter is interesting because it preaches the doctrine of Parinamana (*eko*), the turning over of merit for the salvation of others. Chapter twenty-seven deals with the Vows of Samantabhadra, who plays a most important part in the sutra. He represents the student stage not yet in a perfect state of supreme enlightenment. But the most illuminating chapter of all is the thirty-ninth, which describes the ninth assembly, 'Entering into the Universe', and it is this chapter which makes up the *Gandavyuha*. It deals with belief, understanding, practice and enlightenment, which are after all nothing but one's own mind, and this one mind enters into universality and becomes Enlightenment itself.

Interpenetration is the doctrine taught in the Kegon. When we look at the world in the spiritual light of Vairochana Buddha we see it full of radiance, indeed a world of pure light. Everything in this world is interpenetrating, everything is mutually conditioned and conditioning. All things are one, and that one is the Supreme Reality.

The Buddha feels sorrow for those who do not see this radiant world of his Enlightenment, in which Pure World everything is interpenetrating, and puts forth his activity to help these beings to attain Enlightenment. The Bodhisattvas follow him, and through their own practice of the six Virtues of Perfection (*paramitas*) help suffering beings to attain supreme Enlightenment.

3 THE GANDAVYUHA

The *Gandavyuha* occupies about a quarter of the *Avatamsaka* and is complete in itself. It is the '*Nyuhokkaibon*' chapter on 'Entering into the Universe through the Practice and Vows of

Samantabhadra', and describes the pilgrimage of a youth called Sudhana in his efforts to enter the Dharmadhatu, and his consultation with fifty-three good friends. It is the *Pilgrim's Progress* of Buddhism.

Once Buddha dwelt at Sravasti in the grove of Jetavana in the garden of Anathapindika. In that assembly there were five hundred Bodhisattvas, headed by Samantabhadra and Manjusri. All the members of the assembly were waiting for the Buddha to preach. Then he entered Samadhi (deep meditation), and as soon as he did so the forests of Jetavana suddenly became so wide that they became filled with an inexpressible number of worlds, and Bodhisattvas from the ten quarters came and worshipped the Buddha, composing verses of praise. Buddha caused a ray of light to issue from between his eyebrows and illumined the Bodhisattvas and all the ten quarters of the world, and thereby they were filled with compassion to benefit all beings.

Manjusri went out from the Pratisthana to the human world and preached the Mahayana doctrine to many people. While he was staying in the city of Dhanyakara there was in his audience a handsome youth of noble family, Sudhana. While Sudhana was listening with the desire to learn, lead, and perfect the life of a Bodhisattva, Manjusri, looking over the audience, perceived him and knew his aspiration, so he advised him thus: 'You must find a true friend to help you in your search. Go to Myoho Mountain in the country of Shoraku and there you will find a Bhikshu Sagaramegha (*Tokuun*). He will give you good advice.'

Sudhana visited Sagaramegha, who taught him wisely and then sent him on to another friend. In this way he was sent from one friend to another until he had visited fifty-three. At last he came to Samantabhadra, under whose teaching he perfected his vow and entered into the Dharmadhatu (Supreme Reality).

In this story of Sudhana, Samantabhadra plays the chief part as master and Manjusri as the guest, and the activity of both is represented by the youth Sudhana, who visits fifty-three good friends seeking advice and finally attains entrance to the Dharmadhatu. It is the story of Enlightenment, of 'entering into the universe' by means of the practice and vows of the religious life of Samantabhadra.

What kind of persons were the friends Sudhana visited? If we classify them we find that there were five Bodhisattvas, five monks, one nun, eight householders, a physician, a perfume seller, a sailor, two kings, two laymen, four laywomen, three of whom were ladies and one a heavenly maiden, several children, a number of deities, a mendicant, a hermit, and two Brahmins, thus showing the Mahayana tendency to lay stress upon lay people rather than upon monks, of whom there were only five. During his pilgrimage Sudhana was seeking truth without, by asking the help of others, but after passing through many experiences, mental and spiritual, he realised that true knowledge must come from within. The fifty-third friend was Maitreya, who directed Sudhana to go to Manjusri to ask about the law by which he could enter into Samantabhadra's religious life.

The last volume of the sutra is devoted to Samantabhadra's Ten Vows and the desire to be born into Sukhavativyuha (that is, the Pure Land).

The Ten Vows of Samantabhadra are: (1) To worship the Buddhas; (2) to praise the Tathagatas; (3) to make offerings to all the Buddhas; (4) to confess past sins; (5) to rejoice in the virtues and happiness of others; (6) to request Buddha to preach the Law; (7) to request Buddha to live in this world; (8) to study Buddhism in order to teach it; (9) to benefit all beings; (10) to turn over the stock of merit to others.

These vows are the basis of the Bodhisattva's life in Mahayana Buddhism. This last part, concerning Samantabhadra's Vows, has been issued separately, and is known as the *Fugengyogwanbon* ('Practice and Vow of Samantabhadra').

The story of Sudhana is ultimately an epitome of the entire Kegon sutra. In the background is always the Dharmakaya, of which every activity depicted it is really the activity. It is a sutra of Enlightenment and emphasises the fact that all beings can be reborn in the house of the Buddha if they obtain Enlightenment.

4 DASABHUMIKA (JUJI-KYO)

This sutra really forms a part of the *Avatamsaka*, but has been circulated independently. There are two extant translations, one by Dharmaraksha in AD 297, and the other by Kumarajiva. The Sanskrit text of the Sutra still exists. In it a Bodhisattva,

Vajragarbha, explains the ten stages in the path of the Bodhisattva. These are:

1. Pramudita (Joyous). The Bodhisattva in this stage practises compassion according to the teaching of the Paramita Dana, giving.

2. Vimala (Pure). The Bodhisattva in this stage has the quality of loving speech and practises according to the Paramita Sila, morality.

3. Prabhakari (Brilliant). The Bodhisattva in this stage meditates upon the reality of things and seeks to find the Law for suffering beings. In this stage he practises the Paramita of fortitude or patience (Kshanti).

4. Arismati (Blazing Fire). In this stage the Bodhisattva exterminates all his false ideas and practises the Paramita of Virya, diligence or energy.

5. Sudurjaya. In this stage the Bodhisattva perfects his knowledge and practises the Paramita of Dhyana, Meditation.

6. Abhimukta (to see face to face), in which the Bodhisattva understands the meaning of the Twelvefold Chain of Causation. In this stage the Paramita Prajna, wisdom, is to be practised.

7. Durangama (difficulty to go), in which he realises and practises the wisdom of Skilful Means (*hoben, upaya* in Sanskrit).

8. Acala (Immovable). In this stage he abides in the condition of neither birth nor death, but enters the Buddha's religion, purifying his Buddha-land, and he practises the Paramita of Parinamana (Turning-over Merit).

9. Sadhumati (Good Mind). Here his wisdom is perfected, and he is able to preach the Law and cause beings to awake to enlightenment. In this stage he practises the Bala (Power) Paramita.

10. In the tenth stage he is seated upon a great lotus and a great light proceeds from him; he is surrounded by the Buddhas of the ten quarters and he himself enters into the centre of the Buddha-land; the ten powers are perfected by him and he becomes a Tathagata. Wisdom (Jnana) is the Paramita he practises in this stage. We must notice in this sutra that the Bodhisattva is praised in contrast to the Pratyekabuddhas and the Sravakas, and that compassion is emphasised and placed

above all. Nirvana appears everywhere; the true nature of things is explained; more than one Buddha is recognised, and householders or lay Bodhisattvas are frequently mentioned. These points are peculiar to Mahayana.

5 VIMALAKIRTI NIRDESA (YUIMA-KYO)

This Sutra has Prajna as its background and is a favourite in the Zen sects.

There were seven translations into Chinese, only three of which are extant. Shotoku Taishi wrote a commentary upon it, and many other commentaries have been written by scholars of Tendai, Kegon, Hosso and Zen. It has been translated twice into English, by Kakishi Ohara in the pages of the *Hannsai Zashi*, in 1899, and also by H. Izumi, in the *Eastern Buddhist*, 1926–8. It has much in common with the Avatamsaka, and stress is laid upon the fact that Buddha's path is identical with this life. Our life is a manifestation of Shinnyo, and the variety of this life is the Pure Land. Moreover, the practice of Buddha's path is not only for monks and nuns but for lay people. Buddha's seed can even be found in the life of passions. The true meaning of the Sutra is to find Buddhahood within ourselves, filled with passions as we are, and then to purify ourselves.

The sutra has a famous character, Vimalakirti (Yuima), a householder Bodhisattva. At a certain assembly of the Buddha Vimalakirti was not present on account of sickness, so Buddha asked various Bodhisattvas to go to inquire after his illness, but one and all declined on the ground that they were not worthy, giving specific instances of his wisdom and virtue. At last Manjusri undertook to go. In answer to his question as to his health, Vimalakirti replied in famous words: 'The sickness of a Bodhisattva comes from great compassion, and exists in the time of ignorance which is possessed by every being. When the sickness of every being is ended, then my sickness will also end. I am sick because beings are sick.' Then Vimalakirti answers many questions of Manjusri, explaining the true principles of Mahayana Buddhism.

The sutra lays stress upon the idea that it is not necessary to be a monk or a nun in order to be a Bodhisattva and live the Bodhisattva life.

6 SURANGAMA SAMADHI (SHURYOGONSAMMAI-GYO)

The plan of this sutra is similar to that of Vimalakirti, but emphasis is laid upon the power of Samadhi by which Enlightenment is obtained. There were nine translations, but all save one (by Kumarajiva) have been lost. The sutra explains the practice of the meditation on Emptiness. The Bodhisattva Sthiramati questions the Buddha as to what Samadhi should be practised by a Bodhisattva who wishes to show forth the life of a Bodhisattva, but does not wish to enter into Nirvana. According to the sutra, the meditation thereafter explained by Buddha is the object of a Bodhisattva who has reached the tenth stage, and by means of it anyone, lay or priest, man or woman, may enter into Nirvana without abandoning the life of birth and death.

7 SADDHARMA PUNDARIKA (MYOHORENGE-KYO, HOKKEHKYO)

No other sutra so connects the Buddhism of China and Japan. Tendai and Nichiren depend entirely on this sutra, and it has influenced Japanese Buddhist teaching in other sects as well. In all Zen temples it is recited daily. It is considered as the most important sutra in Japan and China and has become an object of reverence, because it is considered to be the last and supreme teaching of the Buddha. The twenty-fifth chapter, the Fumonbon (Avalokitesvara homage), is important from the standpoints both of religion and art. There are three extant Chinese translations: (1) By Dharmaraksha (AD 286), (2) by Kumarajiva (AD 406), and (3) by Jisanagupta and Dharmagupta (AD 601), of which Kumarajiva's is the best, and there is a Commentary written by Shotoku Taishi.

The Sanskrit text has been translated into French by M. E. Burnouf, and into English by H. Kern. There is also a partial translation by W. E. Soothill from Kumarajiva's Chinese, and a complete translation by W. E. Soothill and Buno Kato.

At one time Buddha was staying on Grihakuta mountain. In

the assembly were many Bhikshus, Bodhisattvas, devas and other beings. Buddha preached the doctrine and then entered into *samadhi*, and delivered a ray of light which illumined the Eastern world. When Buddha awakened from his meditation he told Sariputra that it was only *hoben*, 'skilful means', that caused him to preach different doctrines because of his compassion for beings. His true teaching is that there is only one vehicle (*yana*) of Buddhist teaching, and that it is for all. Buddha told a story about a father who saved his three children from a burning house by the device of promising them each a carriage (*yana*), pulled by a sheep, a deer, and a cow respectively, and when they emerged they found one splendid carriage. This parable shows how the Tathagata saves all beings from the triple world of a burning house by the use of expedients.

The sutra also expounds the teaching of the external Dharmakaya Buddha, of which Sakyamuni was a manifestation. The eternal Buddha always dwells on Mount Grihakuta and speaks from eternity to eternity, guaranteeing Buddahood to all beings. The twenty-fifth chapter is the Fumonbon, popularly known as Kwannon-gyo (*Samanthamukha*) in praise of the Bodhisattva Avalokitesvara (Kwannon). It tells of the thirty-two bodies used by this Bodhisattva for the sake of serving beings, and of the merit acquired by honouring him and praising him.

8   SRIMALADEVI (SHOMANGYO)

This sutra was translated by Gunabhadra (AD 420–79) and by Bodhiruch (AD 508–35). It was a favourite of Prince Shotoku Taishi, who wrote a commentary upon it. The chief character of the Sutra is a woman, the Princess Srimala, to whom the Buddha appeared and said: 'As you have comprehended the true nature of the Tathagata you will erect an excellent Pure Land.' Thereupon Srimala took the ten great vows, which are:

(1) Never to violate the discipline; (2) not to be haughty; (3) not to be angry with anyone; (4) not to be envious of others; (5) not to be jealous; (6) not to be attached to material things; (7) to practise the four acceptances, charity, loving words, benefiting deeds, and working together in order to help others,

and to abide in non-attachment; (8) to free beings from sufferings; (9) to protest against the violation of discipline; and (10) to keep the true Dharma.

Srimala also preached the one vehicle, that is, Mahayana, asserting that all the doctrines which the Buddha proclaimed and taught are for the sake of Mahayana. As Mahayana is the Buddha's vehicle the three vehicles are ultimately one. Enlightenment is the aim and is equivalent to Nirvana, which in turn signifies the Dharmakaya of the Tathagata.

Princess Srimala mentions three beings who can enter the Mahayana way:

(1) He who perfects by himself the deepest Dharma-wisdom;
(2) he who perfects the wisdom of the Dharma of obedience;
(3) he who, though he does not understand wisdom, yet believes in the Tathagata.

The *Gandavyuha* and the *Kishinron* are associated with this sutra, and it is also in harmony with *Vimalakirti, Saddharma Pundarika, Avatamsaka,* and *Nirvana*.

9 BRAHMAJALA SUTRA (BONMO-KYO)

This was translated by Kumarajiva in AD 406, and is a book of Mahayana disciplinary precepts. It is read by all sects, and especially prized by Tendai and Shingon. In ancient days it was greatly venerated and had a great influence upon Japanese Buddhism. Even now the Mahayana discipline is based upon this sutra. The 'ten grave rules', as given in it, are:

(1) Not to kill; (2) not to steal; (3) not to be unchaste; (4) not to lie; (5) not to drink spirituous liquors; (6) not to talk of the faults of others; (7) not to praise oneself; (8) not to be envious; (9) to cherish gratitude to others; (10) to praise the Three Treasures (Buddha, His Order, and His Teaching).

Compare numbers 6–10 with the Hinayana precepts: Not to eat food in the afternoon; not to sit on a high seat; not to listen to music or attend the theatre; not to use perfumes, and not to possess gold or silver (money). It will be seen that the spirit of the two sets is quite different. The Hinayana precepts refer only to self, and are connected with the body, while Mahayana discipline concerns others and relates to the mind and spirit.

A son of Buddha with a compassionate mind should think of all men as his father and all women as his mother, for these beings in the past have been his parents. If he kills them it is as if he were killing his parents. Even if animals are being killed or suffering, every means should be taken to deliver them.

The last words of the Sutra are these:

One who clings to self and form cannot believe in this sutra. If an aspirant to Enlightenment wishes to make the bud of Enlightenment grow and illumine the world with brightness, he ought to meditate on the true nature of things. As to the true nature of things, it is not born nor annihilated, not one, not different, not coming, not going. In regard to the learned and ignorant there ought not to be any attachment or discriminating thought. Discrimination must be done away with; this is the aim of Mahayana.

This sutra is related to the *Avatamsaka*, for the chief Buddha is Vairochana and the land is the lotus world. It also bears a relation to the *Nirvana Sutra*, for it has the same ideas about Buddhahood being in all beings, and the Dharmakaya as omnipresent and eternal.

10 SUKHAVATI VYUHA (MURYOJU-KYO)

The Prajna Paramita displayed the theory of Emptiness, and the Buddha and Bodhisattva were stressed in other sutras. But the problem of life after death was not considered. At the time of Nagarjuna there were three streams of rebirth in the Pure Land thought:

(1) Rebirth in the Tushita Heaven of Maitreya; (2) rebirth in the Eastern Land of Akshobhya; (3) rebirth in the Western Pure Land of Amitabha.

These ideas show a progressive development. Even in Hinayana, Maitreya was believed to save beings in this world and take them to his heaven, but the Eastern Land of Akshobhya has a close connection with the *Prajna Paramita Sutras*. To be born there depends upon one's own power, and the Emptiness idea is prominent; in these respects it differs very much from the Pure Land of Amida, for one is born there as a result of His grace.

The first Amitabha text is the *Larger Sukhavati Vyuha*, introduced into China by Shi-kao and Lokakshema in the second century AD; after that several translations were made. That by Sanghavarman, made in AD 252, is largely used by Jodo and Shin followers. It was Kumarajiva, AD 465, who for the first time translated the one known as the *Smaller Sukhavati Vyuha*, which lays great stress on the fact that people can be saved or born in the Land of Bliss if only they remember and repeat the name of the Buddha Amitabha before their death, while the *Larger Sukhavati Vyuha* denies that good works are necessary as a stock of merit.

In the *Larger Sukhavita Vyuha* Sakyamuni is the teacher. The Sutra begins with a dialogue between the Buddha and his disciple Ananda, in which the Buddha tells about the monk Dharmakara (Japanese, *Hozo*), who became the Buddha Amitabha after years of Bodhisattva living and working, and made a vow that he would not obtain the bliss of Buddhahood until all beings were saved. He established his Pure Land for the salvation of man, entrance to it needing only faith in him and his will to save. However, the duration of sojourn in the Pure Land is not eternal, for it is a field for purification and illumination, and a return to this world is possible in order to save others.

There are passages in Nagarjuna's work which foreshadow the Amida doctrine, and it is said that when he died he faced the Western Paradise. He is accordingly regarded in the Jodo and Shin sects of Japan as the first patriarch, Vasubandhu being the second.

The Amida Buddhist literature, however, developed in China, for we do not hear of it in India except for a few passages in the works of Nagarjuna and Vasubandhu, nor do the Buddhist pilgrims, Fa-hien and Hsuan-chuang, mention it. But the spirit of Bhakti was bound to enter the Buddhist religion, and it does so in the form of faith in the Buddha Amitabha and his Pure Land.

11 MAHAPARINIRVANA SUTRA (DAIHATSUNEHAN-GYO)

Hinayana has its Nirvana Sutra, but Mahayana has its own. It was translated by Dharmaraksha in AD 423, this being one of the only two translations extant.

The scene of the sutra is at Kushinara as Buddha is about to enter Nirvana. Buddha asserts the indestructibility of Buddha's body and the nature of the Tathagata, which is righteousness itself. He tells of the Bodhisattva's virtues. He asserts that all beings have the Buddha-nature and that the ten stages of the Bodhisattva's path lead to the highest wisdom. In this Sutra it is shown that Buddha-nature is the cause which develops the effect which is Buddhahood and Nirvana. It asserts that Enlightenment is Nirvana.

That all beings have the nature of Buddha shows the true meaning of self or ego; the self is Tathagata. In Buddha's teaching the ego is nothing but Buddha-nature, and the meaning of no-self is equivalent to the great self, that is to say Buddha.

The three great Mahayana Sutras are said to be *Prajna Paramita*, *Saddharma Pundarika*, and *Nirvana*. Kumarajiva said that *Prajna Paramita* exterminates false views, *Saddharma Pundarika* reveals the ultimate truth, and *Nirvana* preaches the true way. The three sutras are considered the great gates to salvation.

The Nirvana sect based upon this sutra once existed in China, but when Tendai regarded the sutra as the last part of the *Saddharma Pundarika* the Nirvana sect became merged in Tendai.

12 THE LANKAVATARA SUTRA (RYOGA-KYO IN JAPANESE, LING-CHIA-CHING IN CHINESE)

The *Lankavatara Sutra* is one of the most important Mahayana texts, especially as related to the development of Zen in China. It was first translated into Chinese between 412 and 433 by an Indian Buddhist scholar called Dharmaraksha. This translation is now lost. The second, by Gunabhadra in AD 433, is the earliest extant. Bodhidharma, who came to China in 520, is said to have given this text to his disciple Hui-k'e as containing the essence of his teaching. The *Lankavatara*, however, is a sort of notebook kept by a Mahayanist who recorded in it all the major ideas belonging to his school. If we wish to take it for a textbook of any definite school of Mahayana Buddhism it must be that of the Avatamsaka, for the chief idea running through it is not that of consciousness-only but that of Mind-only; and we must know how to make a distinction between these two thoughts. Consciousness or Vijnana, as conceived by the Yogacara doctrine, is subjective and individual, while Mind or Citta, according to the *Avatamsaka* and the *Lankavatara*, is transcendental, that is, beyond dualistic ideas. In Mind are included both the thinker and the thought, whereas in Yogacara's consciousness the so-called objective world has no existence.

The *Lankavatara* is mystical in the sense that it speaks of our experiencing a complete spiritual regeneration called *Paravritti*. This is the 'turning-about' of our entire personality whereby the original Buddha-nature, here called the Tathagatagarbha (the Tathagata's womb), reveals itself. This phenomenon may be called a spiritual revolution leading to Enlightenment.

This inner experience, logically speaking, disposes of all forms of 'false judgement' (*parikalpa*), which is the outgrowth of not seeing things as they are. Paravritti corrects this, and thereby enables us to exercise the 'wisdom of non-discrimination' to its fullest extent. This wisdom is Enlightenment.

The *Lankavatara* is closely connected with Asvaghosha's *Awakening of Faith*, most of the major subjects treated in the latter being also those of the former.

13   VAJRASEKHARA SUTRA (KONGOCHO-KYO)

This sutra, together with the Dainichi-kyo, is used by the Tendai and Shingon sects, the former stressed by Tendai and the latter by Shingon. According to Tibetan tradition the *Kongocho-kyo* was circulated in India in the last part of the seventh century. At the beginning of the eighth century it was introduced to China by Kongochi. The *Kongocho-kyo*, in its three-volume form, was transmitted to Japan by Kobo Daishi in AD 806.

The original sutra is very long, but the sutra read and taught at the First Assembly is the most fundamental and important.

This sutra explains the esoteric teaching of Shingon. It is difficult to give an outline of it to the general reader, for certain knowledge and appreciation of Shingon esoteric teaching is necessary in order to understand it. The general import of it, however, is to explain the realisation of Buddhahood.

14 KISHIN-RON – MAHAYANA-SRADDHOPADA-SASTRA

Besides the sutras there are *sastras* and commentaries upon the sutras, some of these being of great importance. Probably the most outstanding *sastra* is the *Kishin-ron (sraddhopada)*, called in English the '*Awakening of Faith in the Mahayana*', by Asvaghosha. The Sanskrit original is lost, but there are two existing Chinese translations, one by Paramartha (AD 554), and another by Sikshananda (AD 700), and two English translations, by D. T. Suzuki (Chicago, 1900) and by Timothy Richard. D. T. Suzuki says that this book is of paramount importance as being the first attempt to systematise the fundamental thoughts of Mahayana Buddhism, as well as forming a main authority for all Mahayana schools.

The three most important points in this *sastra* are: (1) The conception of Suchness (*bhutatathata*), (2) the Three Bodies of the Buddha (*trikaya*), and (3) Salvation by Faith.

Suchness (*bhutatathata, shinnyo*) is the essence of the Mahayana, but relatively it becomes *Samsara* (birth and death) through the law of causation. Shinnyo is the great all-including whole, which appears as particularity, but in its essence remains pure and undefiled. It has two aspects, Bhutatathata and Samsara, which are so closely related that they are really two different views of One Reality; hence the Mahayana statement that Nirvana and Samsara are the same, which many find a difficult point to accept in Mahayana philosophy. Bhutatathata is that which is neither existence nor non-existence – it is *empty* of particularity. Samsara is this life of relativity, but when it is divorced from particularity it is found to mean the same as Bhutatathata. Bhutatathata is the substance of the universe, the Absolute and Infinite. The relation between Suchness and Phenomenality is the Aralashiki (*alaya-vijnana*), which has two aspects, Enlightenment and Ignorance.

As Mind is pure in its essence, how does Ignorance come

forth? The *Kishin-ron* explains that this Pure Mind is stirred by Ignorance, or perfumed by it, and while this perfuming does not affect its true nature, it acts as a cloud to obscure it. This perfuming by Ignorance through activity creates an illusory mind, which gives rise to passions and attachments, which in turn produce suffering. But as Ignorance perfumes Suchness and Suchness impresses Ignorance we have the power to attain Enlightenment, and the true meaning of Dharmakaya is revealed. This is the essence of this *sastra*, to understand the meaning of Suchness and Samsara and its relation to Ignorance and Enlightenment. It also includes practical advice in regard to acquiring faith, leading the good life, and practising meditation and right contemplation.

PART TWO

Chapter 6

Extracts from Mahayana Sutras

GENERAL TEACHING OF THE BUDDHAS

Do not commit evils;
Perform good deeds;
Purify your own thought;
This is the teaching of the Buddhas.

Nehan-gyo (Nirvana-sutra)

This is Buddha's doctrine; not to cherish enmity, not to fight, not to abuse.

Hozo-kyo (Ratnakarandakavyuha-sutra)

For Buddhas there is only one thing to do; to benefit all the world, to purify the world, and to exterminate unrighteousness. This is the reason for their appearance.

Daihotodarani-kyo (Pratyutpa-Buddha-
sammukhavasthita-samadhi-sutra)

The Tathagatas with endless compassion sympathise with the Triple World. They appear in this world in order to propagate the doctrine and to save and benefit beings.

Muryoji-kyo (Sukhavati-vyuha)

TRUE NATURE OF ALL THINGS

Truth means that which is not falsehood, that is, Shinnyo (*tathata*). The true essence of all things is absolute identity with Shinnyo. Shinnyo is beyond all relativity, evil and passion. By its nature it is pure, tranquil, permanent, unchanging.

Transmigration is a wilderness, Passion is thirst.

Buddha and Bodhisattva are the good means to help us to discern the Trust (Reality or Shinnyo).

Ho-u-kyo (Ratnamegha-sutra)

Buddha spoke to the Bodhisattva Tokuhon; 'O Tokuhon, there are three aspects in all things.

1   All names of things are provisionally established; according as objects rise they are provisionally established; as objects arise they are described in words; and all beings become attached to them (as real).

2   All things are born of causation, that is, ignorance causes karma until it brings about a great aggravation of suffering.

3   Although all things appear differentiated they are in substance of sameness and suchness, that is, of the true nature of Shinnyo. When we know the substance we return to the original nature of all things.

The first case is like one having a film over the eye. The second case is like one who has trouble through seeing things and forms which do not exist. But the third case is like one who has the pure eye free from trouble and sees well into the original nature.'

Gejinmitsu-kyo (Sandhinirmocana-sutra)

There is no moon in the water; the moon is seen reflected there with pure water as occasion (*pratyaya*). All things are born of causation and phenomenal, but ignorant people cling to them as real.

Shinjikwan-gyo (Mulajata-hridaya-bhumi-dhyana-sutra)

The true nature and the true form of all things are permanent and never change.

Kegon-kyo (Avatamsaka-sutra)

THE MIND

In Buddhism, Mind is of the greatest importance; all things depend upon it and are never outside it.

Shinjikwan-gyo (Mulajata-hridaya-bhumi-dhyana-sutra)

Mind is like a clever artist; it paints all worlds, and out of it rise the Five Aggregates. When a man knows that the Mind is the creator of worlds he sees the Buddha, he knows the true nature of Buddhahood, because Mind, Buddha, and Beings are the same. When a man wishes to understand all the Buddhas of the past, present, and future, he should meditate that it is the Mind which creates all the Tathagatas.

Kegon-gyo (Avatamsaka-sutra)

The Mind is the leader of all things. When a man understands the Mind he knows all things, because all things of the world are created by the Mind.

Hannya-kyo (Prajnaparamita-sutra)

It is by the Mind that the triple world is understood. It is so with the Twelvefold Chain of Causation. Even birth and death are caused by the Mind, and when it is quieted there is no more birth and death.

Kegon-gyo (Avatamsaka-sutra)

When the Mind is disturbed the multiplicity of things is produced; when the Mind is quieted the multiplicity of things disappears. In spite of defilement the Mind is eternal, clear, pure and not subject to transformation.

Kishin-ron (Mahayana-sraddhotpada-sastra)

Manjusri asked Buddha, 'What is the Mind? Preach it for the sake of beings who are not yet enlightened.'

Buddha answered, 'You are really a mother, Manjusri, for you ask this question for the sake of those beings who have first awakened the desire for enlightenment. The Tathagatas deem the Mind as the supreme Dharma of Buddha; it benefits all beings, extinguishes evil karma, helps beings to cross over the danger of transmigration, and keeps calm the ocean of suffering. In the triple world the Mind is supreme master, and he who meditates upon this obtains Nirvana. Nothing really exists in the triple world but the Mind, which is like the earth from which all things grow. You ought to join with good friends and hear the doctrine of Mind, meditate upon the doctrine, and practise to attain supreme enlightenment.'

Shinjikwan-gyo (Mulajata-hridaya-bhumi-dhyana-sutra)

TRANSIENCY

All the worlds are like a flickering flame; they are like a shadow, an echo, a dream; they are like a magical creation.

Yuima-kyo (Vimalakirti-nirdesa)

BUDDHA-NATURE

The human mind possesses the Buddha-nature unobtainable from others. It can be compared to a man who has a jewel in his clothes he knows not of, or to a man who seeks after food when he has a treasure in his own storehouse.

Shuryogon-kyo (Surangama)

All beings are capable of acquiring great faith, for it is taught that they are all in possession of the Buddha-nature.

Nehan-gyo (Nirvana-sutra)

The nature of the Mind of all beings is pure and cannot be stained by passions; it is like the sky which can never be tainted.

Daishu-kyo (Mahasannipata-sutra)

When Mind is separated from defilements, I preach it to be the Buddha.

Ryoga-kyo (Lankavatara-sutra)

The Bodhisattva is enlightened in his own mind, which is also the Mind of all beings. When his mind is pure the mind of all beings is also pure, for the substance of one Mind is that of all beings. When the dust of one's own mind is thoroughly wiped off, all beings also have their minds free from dust. When one's mind is freed from greed, anger, and folly all beings are also freed from greed, anger and folly. Such a Bodhisattva is known as the All-knowing One.

Daishogonhomon-gyo (Manjusri-vikridita-sutra)

MIND IS THE ORIGIN OF SIN

The mind is easily upset and runs wild and is difficult to keep controlled. When it runs wild it is like a violent elephant; one thought follows another with the quickness of lightning; when the mind loses its composure it moans like an agile monkey and thus becomes the origin of all evils.

Nehan-gyo (Nirvana-sutra)

The great river of passions drowns all beings of the triple world. A Bodhisattva alone can cross to the other shore by the practice of the Six Paramitas.

Nehan-gyo (Nirvana-sutra)

The poison of poisons is the three passions of greed, anger, and ignorance.

Nehan-gyo (Nirvana-sutra)

Among the passions greed is the chief because it causes all pain.

Yuga-ron (Yogacaryabhumi-sastra)

One moment of an angry mind burns up the goodness accumulated during immeasurable *kalpas*.

Dainichi-kyo (Mahavairocana-sutra)

Ignorant beings allow themselves to be bound by the five desires, thus giving opportunity to the evil one to carry them away, body and mind, just as a monkey is carried away by a hunter on his shoulder.

Nehan-gyo (Nirvana-sutra)

KARMA

Why do some suffer pain and others pleasure, directly or indirectly, in this world or some other world? The result is according to their karma.

Kegon-gyo (Avatamsaka-sutra)

When a man does not understand the teaching of karma he suffers transmigration for immeasurable periods of time. All things are designed by Mind. Mind paints the passions and passions paint karma and karma paints the Body.

Ubasokukai-kyo (Upasaka-sila-sutra)

Never think when you do evil, 'No one knows.' There are four who know. 1 Heaven, 2 Earth, 3 The Bystander, and 4 Oneself.

Mei-kyo (Sutra Spoken by Buddha on the Thought of Abuse)

When you wish to know about your previous life, know that the life you are living now is the result of it. When you wish to know about your future life, know that the cause of it lies in what you have done in this life.

Ingwa-kyo (*Sutra on the Cause and Effect of the Past and Present*)

TRANSMIGRATION

The Twelvefold Chain of Causation consists of passions, karma, and pain, which mutually become the cause and the effect. From passions karma is produced; from karma pain, from pain passions again. These three condition one another and never stop, like a turning wheel.

Juniinnen-ron (*Pratityasamutpada-sastra*)

THE ORIGIN OF IGNORANCE

When this body is regarded as mine body-karma is produced; when this speech is regarded as mine speech-karma is produced; when this mind is regarded as mine mind-karma is produced. Whereupon covetousness follows, precepts are violated, anger arises, and indolence, distraction, and an evil way of thinking against the Six Paramitas. This is not the way of the Bodhisattvas.

Hannya-kyo (*Prajnaparamita-sutra*)

WAY OF EMANCIPATION

Precept, Meditation, and Wisdom are the way of Emancipation. Precept is to remove the dust of evil deeds, Meditation to remove the dust of bondage, and Wisdom to remove the dust of wrong views.

Gedatsudo-ron (*Vimokshamarga-sastra*)

MEDITATION

Buddha spoke to Mahamati; 'O Mahamati, when you wish to know that all things, inner and outer, are produced by your own mind, separate yourself from noise, sloth, and sleep, and make a thorough survey of all the different aspects of the self-discriminating mind.'

Ryoga-kyo (Lankavatara-sutra)

MODES OF WISDOM

Wisdom grows in three ways; Hearing, Meditating, and Practising.

Hearing is to love the doctrine which one has learned and never to be weary of it.

Meditating is to meditate on all things as they are, considering them as transient, causing pain, empty, and having no self, whereby to loathe them and walk towards the wisdom of the Buddha.

Practising is to be separated from desire and evil thought, and by degrees to enter the way of Enlightenment.

Hotsubodishin-ron (Anuttara-samyaksambodhicittopada-sastra)

BUDDHA AND COMPASSION

Great compassion and a great pitying heart is called Buddha-nature.

Compassion is Tathagata; Tathagata is Compassion.

Nehan-gyo (Nirvana-sutra)

THE BUDDHA-BODY (DHARMAKAYA)

The Buddha-body pervades the universe and manifests itself before all beings according to causality; nowhere is he not found, yet he is immovable from the seat of enlightenment.

Kegon-gyo (Avatamsaka-sutra)

Buddha said to Kashyapa, 'The Body of the Tathagata is permanent and never destroyed; it is the *vajra*-body which is perfected by virtue of the true Dharma of which he is the guardian.'

Nehan-gyo (Nirvana-sutra)

THE BUDDHA-FIELD (BUDDHAKSHETRA)

All Buddhas move in mysterious fields which are beyond comprehension. That is to say, all Buddhas sit in one place, and yet pervade all the worlds, incalculable in number; they preach one phrase of truth in which all the teachings of Buddha are revealed; they emit one ray of light which uniformly illumines all the worlds; they manifest each in his one body all the Buddha-bodies; they reveal all the worlds at one spot; they give in one knowledge a final explanation of all things; they move about in one thought in all the worlds of the ten quarters; they manifest in one thought all the inconceivable virtues and powers of all the Tathagatas; they perceive in one thought all the Buddhas and beings of the past, present, and future, and yet their minds show no sign of disturbance; they identify themselves in one thought with all the Buddhas of the past, present, and future, showing that they are in substance one.

Kegon-gyo (*Avatamsaka-sutra*)

TRANSMIGRATION IS NIRVANA

When enlightenment is perfected a Bodhisattva is free from the bondage of things, but a Bodhisattva does not seek to be delivered from things. Samsara is not hated by him nor Nirvana loved. When perfect Enlightenment illumines, it is neither bondage nor deliverance. Beings by nature are Buddha, so Samsara and Nirvana are like a dream of yesterday. As it is like yesterday's dream there is no birth, no death, no coming, no going.

Engaku-kyo (*Purnabuddha-sutra-prasannartha-sutra*)

A PRECEPT

It is better to hear little and understand the meaning than to hear much and not understand the meaning. One should wish to be a teacher of the mind and not to regard the mind as teacher.

Nehan-gyo (*Nirvana-sutra*)

FAITH

Faith indeed is the son of Buddha, so the wise should strive to be near it.

Hoshaku-kyo (*Maharatnakuta-sutra*)

The message carried by all deeds of merit is faith; of all treasures faith is the best.

Daishogon-kyo (*Lalitavistara*)

ENLIGHTENMENT

Enlightenment is the great road which leads into the city of the all-knowing one. It is the pure eye which can see the way, right and wrong. It is the seed of all the Buddhas and causes all the Buddha-Dharmas to grow.

Kegon-gyo (Avatamsaka-sutra)

When a man recites the name of Buddha with no cowardly heart but with wisdom and straightforwardness he will be in the presence of Buddha.

Junibutsumyo-kyo (Dvadasabuddhaka-sutra)

REPENTANCE

When an evil or a faulty deed is committed, let the doer realise and repent it, and be reformd so as not to repeat it; then the demerit will be daily erased and finally one will attain enlightenment.

Shijunisho-gyo (Sutra of Forty-two Sections)

When one wishes to repent, the Buddhas are invited, sutras recited and vows made for the destruction of all the evil karma committed by one's mind and body; then all sins will be wiped out.

Kwanfugen-gyo (Sutra of Meditation on the Bodhisattva Samantabhadra)

All evils committed in former ages by me were caused by greed, anger, and ignorance, and born of body, speech, and mind. All these I regret and repent.

Kegon-gyo (Avatamsaka-sutra)

A DAILY PRECEPT

Buddha said; 'O Bodhisattva, these are things to be removed by a Bodhisattva; greed, anger, ignorance, self, laziness, sleep, lust, and doubt. Moreover, there is one thing which a Bodhisattva must guard himself against, that is not to advise others to do things which he does not desire for himself.'

Mujihomon-kyo (Anakshara-granthaka-rocanagarbha-sutra)

ROOT OF DESIRE

Of the five sense-organs mind is the master. Therefore you ought to control your mind. Mind is more terrible than a venomous snake, a vicious beast, a great robber or great fire.

> *Yuiko-gyo (Sutra Spoken by Buddha just before his Entering Parinirvana)*

Rather break your bones and heart than commit sins by following your selfish heart. It is not only the bodily strong man who has power; one who controls his own mind is stronger than he. Infinite *kalpas* have passed since Buddha struggled against his mind. He never yielded, and after untiring effort obtained Buddhahood.

> *Nehan-gyo (Nirvana-sutra)*

The nature of mind is pure, but evils are the dust on it. Remove the dust of the mind with the water of wisdom.

> *Monjushurimon-gyo (Manjusri-pariprikkha-sutra)*

PATIENCE

Buddha addressed the assembly and said; 'Patience is the best thing in the world; it is the way to contentment, it comforts solitude, it is honoured by wise men, it cements friendship, it gains fine reputation, it leads to freedom, power, dignity, it illumines the world, it brings skill, it subdues melancholy and enmity, it adds to beauty, it smoothes racial relations, it brings excellent rewards, it works for goodness, longevity, and honour. Patience hurts nobody and is the Buddha-Dharma.'

> *Daishu-kyo (Mahasannipata-sutra)*

DILIGENCE

A Bodhisattva should be diligent so as not to be disturbed by lust, ignorance, haughtiness, annoyance, envy, enmity, hatred, flattery, and shamelessness. A Bodhisattva should always think in this way: I always practise diligence because I do not wish to cause suffering to any beings, because I wish to know all beings and the way they are born and pass away. I practise diligence because I want to know Buddha's true law, have wisdom, and know how to use skilful means in order to procure the happiness of Nirvana for all beings. I practise diligence because I wish to suffer the sufferings of hell for the sake of all beings, so as to make them come to the realisation of Enlightenment.

Kegon-gyo (Avatamsaka-sutra)

CHASTITY

Carnal desire produces the fetters and calamity of the world and causes suffering. When one practises Buddha's Law one is saved from them. Carnal desire is an evil, and one released from a prison has no wish to return to it.

Nichimyobosatsu-kyo (Sutra of Boddhisattva Suryaprabha)

GRATITUDE

To know gratitude is the root of great compassion. It is the gate to open up good deeds and to be beloved by others.

Chido-ron (Mahaprajnaparamita-sastra)

There are four kinds of gratitude:

1   To parents,
2   To other beings,
3   To rulers,
4   To the Three Treasures.

Shinjikwan-gyo (Mulajata-hridaya-dhyana-sutra)

MASTER AND FRIEND

Make a good teacher of compassion. Select a good master and friend. The good friend is to preach the Law as it is and practise according to the Law. He is to practise faith, discipline, charity, wisdom, and cause others to practise them. What is the Good Law? It is everything which is not for selfish pleasure but for the pleasure of all beings.

Nehan-gyo (Nirvana-sutra)

SPIRIT OF CHARITY

A Bodhisattva is a great giver and gives things equally to all beings, seeking no reward. He wishes to save all beings and to understand the true ways of Buddhas. This is the spirit of the Bodhisattva.

Kegon-gyo (Avatamsaka-sutra)

When a man practises charity in order to be reborn in heaven, or for fame, or reward, or for fear, such charity can obtain no pure effect.

Funbetsugoho-kyo (Sutra on the Distinction and Protection of Dharma)

A Bodhisattva abiding in the stage of No-dust is naturally separated from killing of all kinds; he is compassionate to all beings.

Kegon-gyo (Avatamsaka-sutra)

HOW TO BEHAVE IN THIS LIFE

When you see men in disharmony try to create harmony. Speak of good in others and never of their faults. Cherish a good mind even for your enemy. Hold to the mind of compassion and regard all beings as your parents.

Ubasokukai-kyo (Upasaka-sila-sutra)

TO TAKE REFUGE IN THE THREE TREASURES

When a man takes refuge in Buddha with a devoted mind he obtains great happiness, for the mind of Buddha remembers beings by day and night. When a man with devoted mind takes refuge in Dharma he will obtain great happiness, for the power of Dharma by day and by night protects beings. When a man takes refuge in Sangha he will obtain happiness, for the power of Sangha by day and by night protects beings.

Taishakushomon-gyo (Indra-sakra-paripriccha-sutra)

I take my refuge in the Buddha, and pray that with all beings I may understand the Great Way, whereby the Buddha-seed may forever thrive.

I take my refuge in the Dharma, and pray that with all beings I may enter deeply into the sutra-treasure, whereby our wisdom may grow as vast as the ocean.

I take my refuge in the Sangha, and pray that with all beings I may reign in great multitudes and have nothing to check the unimpeded progress of Truth.

Kegon-gyo (Avatamsaka-sutra)

PREACH ACCORDING TO THE CAPACITY OF BEINGS

The Bodhisattva knowing the deeds, causations, and desires of beings preaches the Law according to their capacity. He speaks of purity for the sake of the greedy one, he speaks of mercy for the sake of the angry one. He teaches ignorant ones to investigate all things, and he gives the perfect doctrine of wisdom for those possessed of the three evils. He preaches the three sufferings for the sake of those who find pleasure in Samsara. He preaches tranquillity when he sees beings attached, he preaches diligence when he finds beings idle. He preaches equality to those who cherish arrogance, he preaches the Bodhisattva-mind to those who like to flatter, he makes beings perfect when he finds them blessed in tranquillity.

Kegon-gyo (Avatamsaka-sutra)

THE BODHISATTVA

A Bodhisattva reveals all the activities of this world, is never tired of teaching beings, and manifests himself according to the wish of beings. He is never attached to deeds, and delivers all, manifesting himself sometimes as an ignorant being, sometimes as a holy man, sometimes in the midst of Samsara, and sometimes in the state of Nirvana.

Kegon-gyo (Avatamsaka-sutra)

The Bodhisattva's great compassion is awakened in ten ways; when he sees beings without refuge, when he sees them led into a wicked way, when he observes them poor and without a stock of merit, when he sees them sleeping in the midst of Samsara, when he sees them practising evil, when he sees them bound by desire, when he sees them drowning in the ocean of Samsara, when he sees them suffering incurable diseases, when he sees them showing no ambition to do good, and when he sees them altogether going astray from the Dharma of all Buddhas.

Kegon-gyo (Avatamsaka-sutra)

Chapter 7

Conclusion

1 PERSONS REVERED IN JAPANESE BUDDHISM

Shotoku Taishi (572–621), considered as the founder and establisher of Buddhism in Japan, was the second son of the Emperor Yomei. He was given the name of Umayado because his mother, while walking in the palace grounds, was suddenly seized with the pains of childbirth and her son was born in the Imperial stables (*umaya*). At the accession of his aunt, Suiko (593), he was named heir (*taishi*) to the throne and became the regent. He gave great support to Buddhism, became an earnest disciple, built monasteries, studied and lectured upon the sutras, wrote commentaries on them, promulgated a code of law and compiled two historical works. He is now revered by all classes of people, and by every Buddhist sect. The temple of Horyuji in Nara, the oldest in Japan and a treasure of art, was erected by him, as well as Shitennoji in Osaka and many others.

Shotoku Taishi promoted not only Buddhism but also the political and cultural life of the nation. He was filled with compassion and established dispensaries for the sick and poor and also for animals. His death anniversary is called *Shoryoe*, and is celebrated in April at the temples specially associated with him.

Kobo Daishi (*Kukai*, 774–835) was the founder of the Shingon sect and one of the greatest characters in Japanese religious history. He studied the Secret Doctrine in China and brought its teachings to Japan, where they had great success. He founded many temples, including the famous monastery of Koya. Not only was he a great religious genius but also a poet, painter, sculptor and calligrapher of note. His tomb on Mount Koya is visited by many pilgrims of all sects, and his memory is adored by the followers of Shingon. March 15th is the anniversary of his death.

Dengyo Daishi (*Saicho*, 767–822), was another great Japanese

Buddhist leader. He studied the teachings of Tendai in China, and was the founder of the Tendai sect in Japan, and of the celebrated temple Enryakuji on Mount Hiei, near Kyoto. His death anniversary is June 4th.

Honen Shonin (*Enko Daishi, Genku,* 1133–1212), was the founder of the Jodo Sect in Japan. At first he was a Tendai priest, but he later became converted to the Jodo and had many followers. He built the famous temple Chion-In in Kyoto. His death is remembered on January 25th.

Shinran Shonin (*Kenshin Daishi,* 1174–1268) was also at first a Tendai priest but was converted to the Amida sect by Honen. He established the Jodo Shinshu or True Sect of the Pure Land (*Jodo*), and abolished the differences of living between priests and laymen. The chief temples of the sect are the East and West Hongwanji in Kyoto, with their many branches. His death is commemorated on November 28th.

Eisai Zenji (1141–1215) was a famous Zen priest who visited China twice. At first a priest of Tendai, he later propagated Zen of the Rinzai School, which he had brought from China. He introduced the drinking of tea into Japan. His death anniversary is July 5th.

Dogen Zenji (1200–53) was a disciple of Eisai when both belonged to the Tendai sect. He visited China and later preached Zen according to the Soto school. He was also a famous poet. His death day is August 28th.

Nichiren Shonin (1222–82) was founder of the Nichiren or Hokke sect, which especially reveres the Hokke Sutra (*Saddharma-Pundarika-sutra*). All other founders of Buddhist sects taught doctrines imported from China, but Nichiren is purely Japanese. His followers consider him an incarnation of Bosatsu Jogyo, a disciple of Sakyamuni. His death day is October 13th.

2 BODHISATTVAS REVERED IN BUDDHIST TEMPLES

Kwannon

Kwannon is the Japanese form of Avalokitesvara (Chinese, Kwan-Yin), who is usually represented in Chinese and very often in Japanese Buddhism as feminine. The word Avalokitesvara means the Lord who is seen, and he is often found in a triad with Amida and Seishi (Sanskrit, Mahasthamaprapta), who then represents Wisdom. He is greatly revered by all sects except the Shin, which gives worship only to Amida. He is found chiefly in Tendai, Shingon and Zen temples. There are many forms of Kwannon, and he is often shown with many arms and hands, each hand holding a Buddhist object, and sometimes with several heads. Both the many arms and heads express the idea that Kwannon is always ready to help misery and suffering. A chapter of the *Saddharma Pundarika* is devoted to his praise.

Next to Dainichi and Amida, Kwannon is the most honoured of all Bodhisattvas. He is supposed to be the spiritual son of Amida, and a statue of Amida is often seen on his head.

The most frequent forms of Kwannon are:
1   Sho Kwannon, generally depicted as a beautiful woman, holding a lotus.
2   Juichimen Kwannon with eleven faces.
3   Senju Kwannon with one thousand arms.
4   Bato Kwannon surmounted with a horse's face, as an incarnation of the saviour of animals.
5   Nyoirin Kwannon, seated with the right hand supporting the cheek.

Monju (Sanskrit, Manjusri)
Monju represents wisdom. He is often shown in a triad with Sakyamuni and Fugen, the symbol of mercy or love. He is generally represented riding upon a lion, holding in his right hand a sword with which to cut ignorance, and in his left a sutra believed to be the Prajna-Paramita. He is much revered in the Tendai, Shingon and Zen sects. His statue is generally found in the Zen meditation hall, as the patron of transcendental wisdom.

Fugen (Sanskrit, Samantabhadra)
Fugen, the symbol of love and mercy, presides over Bodaishin (the desire for enlightenment), and is generally represented riding upon an elephant. He is also considered, like Monju, as a Bodhisattva devoted to meditation.

Kokuzo (Sanskrit, Akasagarbha)
Kokuzo also represents wisdom. His statue is found in Tendai,

Shingon and Zen temples and receives much honour among Nichiren worshippers.

Miroku (Sanskrit, Maitreya)
Miroku, now a Bodhisattva, is the coming Buddha. He is the only Bodhisattva of Hinayana Buddhism. In Gandhara figures he is generally represented seated, and in India standing. In Japan he is generally seated and holds a vase or a pagoda. He is considered the king of enlightenment and mercy, but where Kwannon delivers from suffering Miroku confers happiness.

Jizo (Sanskrit, Kshitigarbha)
Jizo is the personification of benevolence, helping all beings in the Six States of Existence, that is, Hell, Hungry Ghosts, Warriors, Animals, Human and Heavenly Beings. He is the patron of travellers and of children. Jizo is represented in the form of a priest with a shaven head. In one hand he holds a jewel, in the other a staff with metal rings. Besides being the object of worship in many temples, his stone image is found on the roads and highways throughout Japan.

There are many other Bodhisattvas, especially in Tendai and Shingon, and a number of Myoos (Sanskrit, Vidyaraja) like the popular Fudo, Benzaiten (Sanskrit, Sarasvati), the deity of art and literature, the Shitenno, the Four Heavenly Kings and many others.

3 BUDDHIST ETHICS

In this brief and simple review of Mahayana Buddhism I have not included a separate chapter or heading for Buddhist ethics, for these are contained in the Paramitas and the Five Precepts,* and therefore do not require separate treatment. A careful study of these, and meditation upon them, will reveal how beings should act in this world of Samsara, and so tread the path of the Bodhisattva which leads to Buddhahood.

---

* The Five Precepts are: (1) Not to kill any living being, (2) not to steal, (3) not to be unchaste, (4) not to lie, (5) not to become intoxicated.

4   ART

I have said nothing about Mahayana and Art, yet the two are closely connected. Early Buddhism, including the Hinayana, did not conceive of art as an adjunct of the Buddhist life, but the Mahayanists soon realised its value and bent their efforts to further their religion through the display of art. Buddhist sculpture and painting as represented by Mahayana artists are not surpassed anywhere.

Spiritual communion between the Buddha or Bodhisattva and his devotee is the Mahayana ideal, and this has resulted in splendid examples of art, in the erection of temples, in the sculpture of beautiful images of the Buddha and Bodhisattvas and in painting of all kinds. Examples are the rock-cut figures of Buddhas and Bodhisattvas in north-west China, and various pagodas erected all over China, most of which are now in ruins. The painting and sculptures of Japan are outstanding, for example the famous statue of Amida Buddha at Kamakura and the equally fine paintings of Amida and the twenty-five Bodhisattvas by Ehin Sozu, now at Koyasan, not to speak of the black and white pictures of Zen artists. In this little book it is impossible to dwell upon this important subject – the close relation between the Mahayana religious consciousness and art, and the results produced – but anyone who is interested in the subject can find the material in books and in reproductions of architecture, sculpture, and painting.

5   ANIMALS IN MAHAYANA BUDDHISM

The Mahayana view about animals is quite different from that of other religions, in which animals are considered as existing only for the use of man and having no rights of their own. However individual animals may be treated in the East, often thoughtlessly and cruelly, it is true, the teaching concerning them in Mahayana is that they also are possessed of the Buddha-nature, and in due time destined for Buddhahood. It is for this reason that their spirits as well as those of human beings are remembered in memorial services for the dead. Just as man has to suffer in this world and often has to sacrifice himself and all he holds dear, so with animals. In this aspect of the universe called Samsara they cannot escape suffering, yet it is our duty as Buddhists to recognise and respect their Buddha-nature and to treat them as kindly as possible.

Not only animals but plants, and indeed all forms of life, possess the Buddha-nature, and in Chinese and Japanese literature we find stories and poems, especially in the Nö plays of Japan, dwelling on the desire for Enlightenment on the part of flowers and plants.

Mercy and compassion in Mahayana Buddhism are to be practised towards all sentient beings, whether human, superhuman or subhuman. In Buddhist teaching we read that the Buddha himself takes the form of an animal when *hoben* (skilful means) seems to require it.

This is a beautiful conception of Mahayana Buddhism. It is to be desired that all Mahayana Buddhists bear it in mind and practise the Paramitas in their thoughts and actions to the outside world, including animals and plants.

6   WHAT MAHAYANA IS NOT

1   It is not polytheism. The various forms of the Buddha, displayed, for example, in the Shingon Mandala, are not gods, but represent the different forms of the One Eternal Buddha.

2   Mahayana is not nihilism. Its conception of the meaning of life, of Nirvana, of the Buddha and of the Bodhisattva is always positive.

3   Mahayana is not a degenerate Buddhism; rather is it a restatement of the Buddha's teaching with different emphasis.

4   Mahayana is not pessimistic, as most Western writers on Buddhism aver. How can a religion be pessimistic which holds out to its followers the conception of the Buddha-nature in all, the principle of a latent Buddhahood which is the possession of every sentient being; of the path of the Bodhisattva who lives to help his fellow creatures; of the possibility of the removal of ignorance and the attainment of Enlightenment when the Truth of the Highest Reality is realised? Mahayana offers salvation to all beings and the opportunity for progress to perfection. How can such a religion be called pessimistic?

The Mahayanist himself is conscious of its doctrine of hope, encouragement and ultimate victory. Mahayana is altruistic and optimistic. The jewel of Truth and Beauty shines in the Lotus and the Mahayanist rejoices and follows the Path.

7 WHAT IT MEANS TO BE A MAHAYANA BUDDHIST

It means to resolve to tread the Bodhisattva path, to strive for Enlightenment, and to work for the welfare of all. It means to live according to Mahayana ethical ideals, which means the practice of the Paramitas:

Dana: Giving, whether in the form of service, love, time, teaching or money.
Sila: Living a life of morality.
Ksanti: Strenuous effort to service.
Dhyana: The practice of meditation.
Prajna: The cultivation of wisdom.

As to doctrine, a Mahayanist may belong to any sect, but the teachings universally held by all are: the law of cause and effect, with the working of karma upon individuals and societies; the fact of suffering and the desire to be released from it; the belief in Non-Ego, in the Buddha-nature, in ultimate Buddhahood and in leading the life of a Bodhisattva by practice of the Paramitas, the Tariki sects stressing faith in Amida and the Jiriki sects stressing Enlightenment through strenuous religious efforts.

Compassion and Wisdom, Enlightenment and the desire to help others – these are the great ideals of Mahayana Buddhism, which can be aspired to by lay people as well as by priests and nuns. It is not necessary to flee from the world to attain Enlightenment. Nirvana and the world of Samsara are but different aspects of the same thing. The Bodhisattva heart may beat beneath a worldly garb, the Bodhisattva spirit manifest itself in worldly life. The quiet life of a monk or nun may intensify certain spiritual experiences; on the other hand, it may produce a tendency to live too much for self-development rather than in fellowship with others.

THE TEACHING OF MAHAYANA BUDDHISM

Enlightenment within rather than without is the goal of Mahayana, for without Enlightenment there is a blind groping in the dark. Yet when Enlightenment comes, compassion will stream forth; men will learn to love their fellow beings; and wars, the exploitation of men and animals, and anger, hatred, and lust will come to an end. This is the teaching of Mahayana Buddhism.

Selected List of Books

RECOMMENDED FOR FURTHER STUDY OF
MAHAYANA BUDDHISM

Anesaki, Masaharu. Buddhist Art in its Relation to Buddhist Ideals. London, 1916.

Anesaki, Masaharu. History of Japanese Religion. London, 1930.

Anesaki, Masaharu. Nichiren, The Buddhist Prophet. Cambridge (U.S.A.), 1916.

Beal, S. Catena of Buddhist Scriptures. London, 1871.

Coomaraswamy, A. K. Buddha and the Gospel of Buddhism. London, 1916.

Coates, N. H., and Ishizuka, R. Honen. The Buddhist Saint. Kyoto, 1925.

Dayal, Har. The Bodhisattva Doctrine in Buddhist Sanskrit Literature. London 1932 (valuable for its information, but on account of its unsympathetic attitude to be read with discrimination).

Dutt, Nalinaksha. Aspects of Mahayana Buddhism and its Relation to Hinayana. London, 1930.

Eliot, Sir Charles. Japanese Buddhism. London, 1935.

Getty, Alice. The Gods of Northern Buddhism. London, 1914.

Goddard, D., and Yamabe, S. Buddha, Truth and Brotherhood, an Epitome of Many Buddhist Scriptures from the Japanese. Santa Barbara, 1935.

Goddard, Dwight. The Buddhist Bible, 1938.

Johnston, R. F. Buddhist China. London, 1913.

Knox, George William. The Development of Religion in Japan. New York, 1907.

McGovern, William M. Introduction to Mahayana Buddhism. London, 1922.

Muller, Max. Buddhist Mahayana Sutras: Sacred Books of the East. Vol. XLIX, Part II (Translations). The Smaller Sukhavati-Vyuha. The Vajracchedikahridaya Sutra. The Larger Prajna. The Smaller Prajna. Oxford, 1894.

Nukariya, Kaiten. Religion of the Samurai. Study of Zen Philosophy and Discipline in China and Japan. London, 1913.

Pratt, James B. A Pilgrimage of Buddhism. New York, 1928.

Radhakrishnan, S. Indian Philosophy. Vol. I, Chaps. X and XII. London, 1923.

Reischauer, August Carl. Studies in Japanese Buddhism. New York, 1917 (written from the standpoint of a Christian missionary but informative).

Reichelt, Karl Ludwig. Truth and Tradition in Chinese Buddhism. Study of Mahayana Buddhism. Shanghai, 1927.

Santideva. Path of Light, Bodhicharyavatara, translation by Lionel D. Barnett. London, 1909.

Saunders, Kenneth. Epochs of Buddhist History. Chicago, 1924.

Saunders, Kenneth. Gospel for Asia. London, 1925.

Schayer, S. Mahayana Doctrines of Salvation. London, 1923.

Shaku, Rev. Soyen. Sermons of a Buddhist Abbot. Chicago, 1906.

Suzuki, Daisetz Teitaro. Asvaghosha's Awakening of Faith in the Mahayana (Translation). Chicago, 1900.

Suzuki, Daisetz Teitaro. Essays in Zen Buddhism, Series I, II, III. London and Kyoto, 1927–33.

Suzuki, Daisetz Teitaro. Introduction to Zen Buddhism. Kyoto, 1934.

Suzuki, Daisetz Teitaro. Manual of Zen Buddhism. Kyoto, 1935.

Suzuki, Daisetz Teitaro. Outlines of Mahayana Buddhism. London, 1907.

Suzuki, Daisetz Teitaro. Studies in the Lankavatara Sutra. London, 1930.

Suzuki, Daisetz Teitaro. The Training of the Zen Buddhist Monk. Kyoto, 1934.

Suzuki, Daisetz Teitaro. The Lankavatara Sutra. London, 1932.

Suzuki, Daisetz Teitaro. Zen and Its Influence on Japanese Culture. Kyoto, 1938.

Soothill, W. E. Lotus of the Wonderful Law. Oxford, 1930.

Steinilber-Oberlin, E. The Buddhist Sects of Japan. London, 1938. Translated from the French.

Thomas, Edward J. History of Buddhist Thought. London, 1933.

Wong, Mow Lam. Sutra Spoken by the Sixth Patriarch. Shanghai, 1930.

Watts, Alan W. The Spirit of Zen. London, 1936.

Yamakami, Sogen. Systems of Buddhist Thought. Calcutta, 1912.

FURTHER BOOKS INCLUDING MATERIAL ON
MAHAYANA BUDDHISM PUBLISHED SINCE
THE FIRST EDITION OF 1938

Benois, H. The Supreme Doctrine. 1955.

Buddhist Mahayana Texts. Translated by Cowell in Sacred Books of the East Series.

Conze, Dr Edward. Buddhism. Its Essence and Development. 1951.

Conze, Dr Edward. Selected Sayings from the Perfection of Wisdom. 1955.

Conze, Dr Edward. Buddhism Wisdom Books. 1958.

Dalai Lama, The. My Land and my People. 1962.

Evans-Wentz, W. Y. Tibetan Yoga and Secret Doctrines. 1935.

Humphreys, Christmas. Concentration and Meditation. 1935.

Humphreys, Christmas. Karma and Rebirth. 1943.

Humphreys, Christmas. The Wisdom of Buddhism (edited). 1960.

Humphreys, Christmas. Zen, a Way of Life. 1960.

Humphreys, Christmas. The Buddhist Way of Life. 1969.

Mehta, Phiroz. The Heart of Religion. 1976.

Murti, T. R. V. The Central Philosophy of Buddhism. 1955.

Pallis, Marco. Peaks and Lamas.

Sangharakshita, Bhikshu. A Survey of Buddhism. 1957.

Schloegl, Dr Irmgard. The Wisdom of the Zen Masters.

Snellgrove, D. Buddhist Himalaya. 1958.

Steinilber-Oberlin, E. The Buddhist Sects of Japan. 1938.

Suzuki, Dr D. T. A new Edition of Outlines of Mahayana Buddhism with a Prefatory Essay by Alan Watts. 1963.

Suzuki, Dr D. T. Myticism, Christian and Buddhist.

Suzuki, Dr D. T. The Zen Doctrine of No-Mind (A Commentary on the Sutra of Hui-neng). 1949.

Suzuki, Dr D. T. Zen and Japanese Buddhism. 1958.

Suzuki, Dr D. T. The Field of Zen. 1969.

Suzuki, Dr D. T. What is Zen? (Contains the Author's 'The Essence of Buddhism' of 1947).

Suzuki, Dr D. T. Shin Buddhism. 1970.

Suzuki, Dr D. T. Japanese Spirituality. Translated by Norman Waddell. 1972.

Trevor, M. H. The Ox and his Herdsman. 1969.

Ward, C. H. S. Buddhism, Volume Two – Mahayana. 1952.

Watts, Alan. The Way of Zen. 1957.

Wong Mou-Lam. The Sutra of Hui Neng. Bound with Price, A. F. The Diamond Sutra.

A Short Glossary of Buddhist Terms

As almost all the words and terms used are clear in the text, it is considered necessary to include only a few in this list.

Abhidharma: The third division of the Pali Tripitaka which consists of an analytical commentary on Buddhist philosophy and psychology.

Agama: A section of Buddhist teaching in Chinese translations belonging to the Hinayana school.

Alayavijnana: The all-conserving consciousness.

Anatta: Non-ego.

Anicca: Impermanence, transience.

Arhat: The ideal saint of Hinayana Buddhism who has realised the highest fruit of ascetic life.

Atman: Soul, Spirit.

Avidya: Ignorance.

Bhikkhu: Member of the Buddhist Sangha or Order.

Bhumi: Stages in the path of the Bodhisattva.

Bhutatathata: Suchness, Reality.

Bodhi: Wisdom, Intuition, Enlightenment.

Bodhicitta: Wisdom, Mind.

Bodhisattva: A being who seeks Enlightenment not only for self but for others.

Citta: Mind, Thought.

Dharani: Holding in Memory, Sacred Formula.

Dharma: Law, Norm, Truth, Religious Teaching, Morality, Existence, Being.

Dharmadhatu: Realm of Ideas, Spiritual World.

Dharmakaya: Body of the Law.

Dhyana: Spiritual Concentration of Mind.

Dukkha: Evil, Suffering, Imperfection.

Hoben: *See* Upaya.

Isvara: A Supreme Personal God.

Kalpa: Immense Period of Time.

Karma: Act, Deed, the Relation of Cause to Effect.

Karuna: Compassion, Love.

Kaya: System, Body.

Nembutsu: A Ceaseless Invocation to Amida Buddha.

Nidana: The Twelve Links in the Chain of Karmic Causation.

Nirvana: The Abode of Ultimate Reality.

Pali Canon: The Tripitaka (Canon) in Pali according to the Hinayana School.

Paramartha: The Highest Truth.

Paramitas: Spiritual Perfections or Virtues.

Parinamana: Transference of Merit.

Prajna: Transcendental Wisdom.

Pranidhana: Vow, Prayer, Self-dedication.

Pratisthana: Abiding.

Pratyeka-buddha: A solitary Buddha who does not announce his truth to the world.

Samadhi: A State of Advanced Enlightenment.

Samsara: The World of Birth and Death.

Sravaka: Hearers, especially in reference to Hinayana Disciples.

Sukhavati: Paradise, the Pure Land of Amitabha.

Sunyata: Emptiness, Void, Reality.

Sutra (Pali, *Sutta*): Sermon or Discourse.

Tathagata: A title of the Buddha meaning 'He who thus comes or goes', that is 'He who has full realisation of the Truth'.

Tathata: *See* Bhutatathata.

Tathatagarbha: The womb where the Tathata is conceived, nourished and matured.

Upaya (Japanese, *Hoben*): Skilful Means, Accommodation, Expediency, Device.

Yathabhutam: Such as it is, in Truth.

Appendix

Twelve Principles of Buddhism
(as drafted by the Buddhist Society, London, in 1945; see Foreword)

1 Self-salvation is for any man the immediate task. If a man lay wounded by a poisoned arrow he would not delay extraction by demanding details of the man who shot it, or the length and make of the arrow. There will be time for ever-increasing understanding of the Teaching during the treading of the Way. Meanwhile, begin now by facing life as it is, learning always by direct and personal experience.

2 The first fact of existence is the law of change or impermanence. All that exists, from a mole to a mountain, from a thought to an empire, passes through the same cycle of existence – i.e., birth, growth, decay and death. Life alone is continuous, ever seeking self-expression in new forms. 'Life is a bridge; therefore build no house on it.' Life is a process of flow, and he who clings to any form, however splendid, will suffer by resisting the flow.

3 The law of change applies equally to the 'soul'. There is no principle in an individual which is immortal and unchanging. Only the 'Namelessness', the ultimate Reality, is beyond change, and all forms of life, including man, are manifestations of this Reality. No one owns the life which flows in him any more than the electric light bulb owns the current which gives it light.

4 The universe is the expression of law. All effects have causes, and man's soul or character is the sum total of his previous thoughts and acts. Karma, meaning action-reaction, governs all existence, and man is the sole creator of his circumstances and his reaction to them, his future condition, and his final destiny. By right thought and action he can gradually purify his inner nature, and so by self-realisation attain in time liberation from rebirth. The process covers great periods of time, involving life after life on earth, but ultimately every form of life will reach Enlightenment.

5 Life is one and indivisible, though its everchanging forms are innumerable and perishable. There is, in truth, no death, though every form must die. From an understanding of life's unity arises compassion, a sense of identity with the life in other forms. Compassion is described as 'the Law of laws – eternal harmony', and he who breaks this harmony of life will suffer accordingly and delay his own Enlightenment.

6 Life being One, the interests of the part should be those of the whole. In his ignorance man thinks he can successfully strive for his own interests, and this wrongly directed energy of selfishness produces suffering. He learns from his suffering to reduce and finally eliminate its cause. The Buddha taught four Noble Truths: (a) The omnipresence of suffering; (b) its cause, wrongly directed desire; (c) its cure, the removal of the cause; and (d) the Noble Eightfold Path of self-development which leads to the end of suffering.

7 The Eightfold Path consists in Right (or perfect) Views or preliminary understanding, Right Aims or Motive, Right Speech, Right Acts, Right Livelihood, Right Effort, Right Concentration or mind development, and, finally, Right *Samadhi*, leading to full Enlightenment. As Buddhism is a way of living, not merely a theory of life, the treading of this Path is essential to self-deliverance. 'Cease to do evil, learn to do good, cleanse your own heart: this is the Teaching of the Buddhas.'

8 Reality is indescribable, and a God with attributes is not the final Reality. But the Buddha, a human being, became the All-Enlightened One, and the purpose of life is the attainment of Enlightenment. This state of Consciousness, Nirvana, the extinction of the limitations of self-hood, is attainable on earth. All men and all other forms of life contain the potentiality of Enlightenment, and the process therefore consists in becoming what you are. 'Look within: thou *art* Buddha.'

9 From potential to actual Enlightenment there lies the Middle Way, the Eightfold Way 'from desire to peace', a process of self-development between the 'opposites', avoiding all extremes. The Buddha trod this Way to the end, and the only faith required in Buddhism is the reasonable belief that where a Guide has trodden it is worth our while to tread. The Way must be trodden by the whole man, not merely the best of him, and heart and mind must

be developed equally. The Buddha was the All-Compassionate as well as the All-Enlightened One.

10 Buddhism lays great stress on the need of inward concentration and meditation, which leads in time to the development of the inner spiritual faculties. The subjective life is as important as the daily round, and periods of quietude for inner activity are essential for a balanced life. The Buddhist should at all times be 'mindful and self-possessed', refraining from mental and emotional attachment to 'the passing show'. This increasingly watchful attitude to circumstances, which he knows to be his own creation, helps him to keep his reaction to it always under control.

11 The Buddha said: 'Work out your own salvation with diligence.' Buddhism knows no authority for truth save the intuition of the individual, and that is authority for himself alone. Each man suffers the consequences of his own acts, and learns thereby, while helping his fellow men to the same deliverance; nor will prayer to the Buddha or to any God prevent an effect from following its cause. Buddhist monks are teachers and exemplars, and in no sense intermediates between Reality and the individual. The utmost tolerance is practised towards all other religions and philosophies, for no man has the right to interfere in his neighbour's journey to the Goal.

12 Buddhism is neither pessimistic nor 'escapist', nor does it deny the existence of God or soul, though it places its own meaning on these terms. It is, on the contrary, a system of thought, a religion, a spiritual science and a way of life, which is reasonable, practical, and all-embracing. For over two thousand years it has satisfied the spiritual needs of nearly one-third of mankind. It appeals to the West because it has no dogmas, satisfies the reason and the heart alike, insists on self-reliance coupled with tolerance for other points of view, embraces science, religion, philosophy, psychology, ethics and art, and points to man alone, as the creator of his present life and sole designer of his destiny.

PEACE TO ALL BEINGS